Warrior Sister,

CUT YOURSELF FREE

from Your Assault

JENIFER DEBELLIS

LIBRARY TALES PUBLISHING
www.LibraryTalesPublishing.com
www.Facebook.com/LibraryTalesPublishing

For general information on our other products and services, please contact our Customer Care Department at 1-800-754-5016, or fax 917-463-0892. For technical support, please visit www.LibraryTalesPublishing.com

Library Tales Publishing also publishes its books in a variety of electronic formats. Every content that appears in print is available in electronic books.

978-1-956769036
978-1736241851

PRINTED IN THE UNITED STATES OF AMERICA

PRAISE FOR *WARRIOR SISTER, CUT YOURSELF FREE*

"As a practicing emergency psychiatrist, I am always looking for informed resources to help trauma victims in their recovery and growth. Jenifer DeBellis's *Warrior Sister, Cut Yourself Free from Your Assault* is the volume I've been waiting for—a compassionate, insightful and systematic guide for girls and young women who refuse to let themselves be defined by their assaults. By incorporating her personal experiences alongside cutting edge techniques from psychology and behavioral health, DeBellis offers an intimate and hopeful book that holds the potential to vastly improve the lives of its readers. An essential tool for both trauma survivors and their providers."

—Jacob M. Appel MD, Associate Professor ofPsychiatry, Icahn School of Medicine at Mount Sinai.

* * * *

"Not only did Jenifer DeBellis overcome her own multiple assaults replete with all the doubts and self recriminations our phallocentric culture sadly supports, but she has produced a brilliant, beautifully written, page-turner: a manual, what she calls a "restoration journey," that will help others work through their trauma as well. If I was still a practicing psychotherapist, several copies of *Warrior Sister, Cut Yourself Free…* would occupy a prominent place in my waiting room."

—Charles W. Brice, Ph.D., author of *The Broad Grin of Eternity* and *All the Songs Sung.*

"Poet, podcaster, and activist Jenifer Debellis is a fresh and important voice in the physical and sexual trauma space. Her stunning observations and eye-opening suggestions in *Warrior Sister, Cut Yourself Free from Your Assault*, are insightful, precise, and need to be on everybody's to-be-read list this year."

—Heather Christie, author of *What the Valley Knows and The Lying Season*.

* * * *

"How does one address the trauma of physical and sexual assault in an engaging, inspiring way? Author, survivor Jenifer DeBellis has managed just that in an insightful, empathetic guide outlining concrete recovery strategies for young adult woman. At times she writes in the voice of a trusted friend sharing her own experiences, often with compelling, relatable analogies. *Warrior Sister, Cut Yourself Free from Your Assault* is a thoughtful, well researched self-help book with the perfect marriage of intellect and compassion. From her modification of the stages of grief, 'Eight Stages of Assault Grief,' to her 30-Day Restoration Journey, this remarkable book will certainly change lives."

—Diane DeCillis, author of *When the Heart Needs a Stunt Double*.

* * * *

"An invaluable survival tool to help girls navigate their way to self empowerment. I hope it gets in the hands of every young woman who needs help finding the light— her light."

—Liz Ferro, founder and author of *Girls with Sole* and *Finish Line Feeling*.

"Jenifer's deep dive into the 8 stages of assault grief, followed by a detailed roadmap to navigate recovery in her 30-day restoration journey is an essential resource for assault survivors. I was inspired by Jenifer's authentic voice as a survivor herself, her story brimming with hope toward a bright future, free from the nightmares of the past. I, too, am a sexual assault survivor and look forward to implementing her Recharge 7-Day Journey into my weekly routine."

—Ally Shaw, Author of *Chasing Tigers in the Dark, Life Lessons of a Fierce Survivor.*

* * * *

"With deep compassion and positivity, author, Jenifer DeBellis, draws on her experiences with sexual trauma and coaching others who have experienced it to empower her readers to break free of the bonds that may be holding them back from living their fullest lives, becoming their most authentic selves. In addition, she looks to research to reinforce the foundation of her "Thirty-Day Restoration Journey," which begins with the affirmation, "I am not defined by my assault." This slim volume is a trove of resources and possible solutions for anyone, particularly young and new women, who have experienced assault. I'm sure this book will help many, many people."

—Kim Suhr, MFA, author of *Nothing to Lose* (Cornerstone Press, 2018) and director of Red Oak Writing.

Special thanks to my life partner, Nick, who was my patient and eager first reader—well listener is more like it. Thanks to my daughters—Catrina, Elisabeth, and Angelina—whose sisterhood is my lifeline and whose own insights inspired so many elements within these pages. Many thanks to Debbie Merion, whose advice on the title, book scope, and future related projects has been invaluable. Thanks to Jen Anderson, whose mad editing skills helped masterfully shape the final version. To all you beautiful souls I've coached and ministered to through your own trauma, thank you for blessing me with your trust, trusting me with your struggles, and sharing your breakthroughs. Thanks, academia, for laying me off three winters ago so I could sit by the fire and write the first draft. Thanks, Library Tales Publishing, for believing in this book and its power to transform lives. And a final thanks to God, who guided me through some tough terrain and trauma and whose gentle voice nudges me to help other survivors navigate their own recovery journeys.

aRIFT+

Assault Recovery Initiatives for Teen Girls & Young Women

Warrior Project

rift | *rĭft*
noun. 1. a deep fracture, crack, or opening in something solid.

For restoration to occur, survivors must move forward from the incident that fractured them. *Warrior Sister, Cut Yourself Free from Your Assault*, in collaboration with aRIFT+ Warrior Project, offers recovery initiatives designed to help assault survivors separate themselves from their assault and assailant to promote self-restoration.

TABLE OF CONTENTS

INTRODUCTION

Shortly after I launched my first book—my debut poetry collection, *Blood Sisters* (Main Street Rag, 2018)—I had an extraordinary, life-altering encounter. I was a featured reader at a Detroit Public Library event. It was one of those venues that included an eclectic cast of poets and authors. Which meant there wasn't a single thread between our topics or styles to weave from one reader to the next. This gave me an idea. Rather than use my entire time slot to strictly read from my new book, I left myself enough time in between pieces to give brief backstory for the coming-of-age narratives I shared. The poems I read centered on growing up in a struggling working-class home and the physical and sexual assault I experienced *and* witnessed. Why I felt compelled to read these exact pieces and share details about them wasn't clear to me at the time. In the final moments of the event, clarity came and found me in the form of a fifteen-year-old girl.

Our encounter was brief, but its impact on me was permanent. What was set into motion following our clipped conversation tattooed a purpose on my soul. I felt the sting of its imprint when, just seconds after

1

our introduction, the teen said, "Thanks for reading those poems. They really spoke to me." She held out her scabbed wrists. "I've survived several sexual assaults and just got out of the hospital after my third suicide attempt." If that didn't just kick you in the gut the way it did me, then your stomach is way stronger than mine, and I have a strong stomach. "Well, I'm glad you didn't succeed," I said. "I know that dark place. It feels hopeless when you're in it, but I can assure you the light is just beyond it." She sniffled and wiped her nose. "Yeah." She nodded. "Yeah. I write through it, you know." And this opened a small window of time for us to rush through some writer talk on writing for therapy, understanding, and release. The whole time we talked, her grandma waved and shouted from the back of the room, "Let's go! Come on, I mean it." We inched our way toward the back, chatting quicker as the seconds slipped from us. "Promise me," I said when her grandma's hand wrapped around her arm, "you'll be good to yourself." "Hey," I added so she'd look back up to my eyes. "I'll try," she sighed. "Promise," I repeated. "I will," she said before she was led away.

There were so many other things I wanted to say to this youngster before her antsy grandma dragged her away. The whole time we talked I kept trying to find a way to jog over to my book bag and gift her a book or my contact info at least. But I knew the moment I turned my back, she'd be gone. I agonized over this failure on my long drive home, apologizing to God for missing this chance to make a real difference in her life. Then repeated these apologies as I fell asleep that night. I resumed my dread and sorry prayers when I awoke the next morning. "Stop it," God's voice filled my headspace. "You did exactly what I wanted you to do." As I prepared my thoughts for the ways I fell short, He cut into them, saying, "Your stories of survival and your witness as a confident woman are your purpose. Don't worry about how I use them."

Now, I don't know if you're a spiritual person or not. But since I am, when God tells me to stop it, I listen. But something had been stirred awake inside my soul that I couldn't ignore. I kept turning *survivor* and *witness* over in my head. My purpose. My purpose. My—the fog lifted a bit around that tattoo on my soul. Assault-recovery initiatives. ARI. The full image came into view: assault-recovery initiatives for teens. a*RIFT*. But what about young women? a*RIFT*$_+$. A rift: a stress crack or fracture in something solid. "a*RIFT*$_+$," I said aloud. Small *a* for assault. *RIFT* in all italicized caps for the survivor who must separate herself from her assault so her total healing can occur. The plus that extends the teen girls and young women age group. *Hm*, I thought, *help young assault victims separate themselves from their assault and attacker so they can move forward and heal.* I might know a few things about this. Okay, I might know quite a few things about this.

A clear vision is great and all. Yet, a vision is only an idea that must be brought to life. My challenge was to figure out how to organize and present this vision, which required a whole other kind of sight and search effort. After some deeper soul-searching and reflection, I realized an assault-recovery initiative outreach must be built on a solid foundation, with tested foundational principals as the mortar that holds it all together. I developed this book as a companion tool for the a*RIFT*$_+$ Warrior Project outreach, events, and blog. I may not know or include everything there is to know about physical and sexual assault. That would be an impossible undertaking. But I *have* learned quite a bit about assault and assault recovery through my own experiences and decades of supporting other survivors through their recoveries. All these experiences were enhanced by the research, trauma-informed training, external support, and resources I discovered along the way.

What I also discovered as I sought answers and solutions are the vast outreaches and resources out there for different types of assaults. The truth is, there are many resources designed for survivors of physical and sexual assault. However, I noticed most were nonspecific with respect to age and gender, which meant their outreach designs and resources end up targeting anyone and everyone with the same considerations and approaches. I also noted many resources were too focused on the type of assault rather than the common emotional impact many survivors endure. This made me wonder: how many sources should a struggling person have to consult to piece together how she is feeling, why she is feeling these ways, and how to deal with it all? How many struggling survivors have the energy, hope, and curious drive to seek the dozen answers they need? I'm willing to bet the number of diligent answer seekers is low. In a fast-paced, tech-savvy world where any answer is a few clicks away, why shouldn't there be one place where the largest demographic of physical violence survivors can find invaluable resources, outreach, and community?

The pages that follow contain my own experiences and insights, a breakdown of the assault grief stages, expert accounts and data on physical and sexual assault, external recovery resources, and an integration of recovery initiatives and challenge options designed to help you move beyond your assault trauma and live in total freedom. I wrote this book for anyone working to overcome physical or sexual assault trauma, with special emphasis on those of you in your late teens and early twenties—that largest demographic of survivors I mentioned above. I wrote this book for you because, as fellow survivors, you should know where to find your sisterhood and how to navigate the valley of recovery that some of us have already made it through. If you're an assault survivor, I hope this book becomes a lifeline and your trustworthy companion. Welcome, warrior sister.

I
PERSPECTIVE *IS* EVERYTHING

"Although the world is full of suffering,
it is also full of the overcoming of it."
~Helen Keller

YOU'RE MORE THAN A STATISTIC

More than 37% of adolescents in the United States are physically assaulted each year, and 9% of them are injured during their assault (CBS News). Roughly 1.8 million minors in the United States have experienced sexual assault. 82% of these victims are female. One in five high school girls report a dating partner has physically and/or sexually assaulted them. Girls between the ages of sixteen and nineteen are three and a half times more likely to fall victim to sexual assault than any other demographic (U.S. Department of Justice). By eighteen, one in four girls will experience sexual assault, and 23.1% of female college undergrads can expect to experience sexual assault initiated by violence, physical force, or while incapacitated (RAINN). These statistics are alarming and show how widespread and mainstream assault against our nation's female youth and new adults is. Worse, these figures only account for reported instances and don't even tap into one of our emergent epidemics: sex trafficking and forced exploitation.

Don't give up all hope for humanity yet. I didn't bring you through all those stats just to devastate you and leave you there. I open with these facts for a few important reasons. First, we should all be aware of the magnitude of physical violence young adults endure. Second, if these statistics match your own experience, you should know you're not alone—not by a longshot. For these reasons, there should be a safe place for assault survivors to seek support, knowledge, and recovery strategies.

Views on speaking up about assault have changed in the last few years. More survivors are breaking their silence about assaults they've endured, which is revealing a much larger community of traumatized girls and young women. Whether you've been physically or sexually assaulted, one detail is constant: you suffered an unlawful bodily attack. Your trauma isn't dictated by the so-called severity or type of your assault. Trauma from an assault is influenced by your emotional response to it, which often can't be controlled. How you process this trauma and recover from it depend on your ability to cope and function while you restore your emotional stability and health.

You are worthy of being 100% emotionally well. If you've experienced an assault and still have some emotional trauma to work through, you could be just a few pages from those breakthrough ideas or plans that will make all the difference in your recovery. Maybe getting a better understanding of the grief stages is exactly what you need at this very moment. It might be the strategies or challenges that will make the biggest impact. Perhaps the additional professional resources and other outreaches are what you need most. Whatever the case, warrior sister, know that you found a sisterhood of fellow survivors who are rooting for you on the sidelines every step of the way.

EVERY STORY HAS A HERO

Sometimes life throws us into situations where we must be our own hero and save our own lost world. The hero's journey is so prevalent in our culture that we see it emerge in blockbuster movie after movie. Take the movie *Alita: Battle Angel* for example. Cyborg Alita confronts a futuristic world left in ruins after a war that devastated Earth. In the unrecognizable metropolis of Iron City, she must fight the powerful who prey on the weak to rediscover her lost identity and restore her world. One of the most striking lines in the movie is when Alita says, "It's the loneliest feeling not to know who you are." To which the scientist, Dr. Dyson Ido, replies, "You'll remember in time." Waking up to face the world after an assault can feel like opening your eyes in a world where your power and identity have been stripped away. You may not know who you are or recognize the face staring back from the mirror. To reclaim your power, restore your identity, and recover your world, you must be willing to do whatever it takes. In this story, you must become your own hero who goes back for the girl and saves her world. It's time to slip into your metal body armor and reclaim your rightful place in your own life.

CONSENT MATTERS NO MATTER WHAT

Growing up, many of the stories I remember began with "Once upon a time" followed by a powerless heroine who needed rescuing—rescuing from her troubles, her world, even herself. Many of the stories my own daughters grew up with had similar storylines. Though this storyline has thankfully been shifting the past decade or so to show more empowered femme heroes taking charge of their own narrative. And although we live in an era that's starting to prioritize the narratives of powerful women, the damsel-in-distress story has done lasting damage. This damage influences our expectations of the hero and his gender. A closer look at some of these earlier exposures will reveal it's usually a female villain wreaking havoc on the heroine's life and a romantic male interest who swoops in to conquer the evil woman and save the day. Consider some princess classics many of us grew up watching like *Snow White*, *Sleeping Beauty*, *Cinderella*, *The Little Mermaid*, and *Tangled*. These stories present women as weak or evil (if they have any power) and the men as the ones who can be counted on to conquer evil and genuinely care for, keep safe, and guarantee the futures of their damsels-in-distress. Yet, heroine stories weren't always presented this way.

In a time long, long ago, heroines were perceived as brave women whose extraordinary courage, accomplishments, and/or qualities were admirable and idealized.

Then someone painted a new face on the heroines we read about or see on stage or screen. The heroines most of us recognize in our lifetime are women who embody noble, virtuous qualities and with whose suffering we're expected to sympathize. It's inherent in these heroines' outcomes that some man in shining armor or with brute strength will rescue her from her demise. Again, it's great to see a shift where many writers and productions aim to realign this narrative mold and present empowered females. Yet, the damsel-in-distress rescue trope is in-grained in many of our romantic minds.

During my young-adult life, I had a Disney princess mindset. It wasn't until later in life I recognized the ro-mantic lie I'd built my entire belief system upon. Around this same time, I recognized another ill-informed belief I held. This was that a woman's NO was negotiable. Many of the protagonists in the fairytales I grew up reading were the same ones in the Disney movies I watched with my young daughters. These female characters were usu-ally thrust into situations they didn't want to be in and their aversions were often dismissed or ignored. Even along their journeys toward self-discovery, these damsels' wishes were ignored or treated lightly if they were en-tertained at all. The message was often that it was more important to be polite than potentially offend someone, especially if this someone was owed gratitude. I started to notice this flawed message as I talked to my daughters and their friends about their autonomy and standing up for themselves when a situation or someone's behavior made them uncomfortable. These conversations not only revealed a shocking truth about how deeply rooted these fairytale ideas were in our minds. They also raised our awareness about storylines and challenged us to seek stories with autonomous heroines we aspired to be like.

Thankfully I've dismantled these unhealthy mind-sets and helped my daughters do the same. An avid reader, I now gravitate toward narratives where the heroine is on a quest of self-discovery and restoration. Many of the protagonists I'm drawn to strive to maintain or (re)claim their autonomy. Many of these protagonists are also assault survivors. Though it feels almost blasphemous to choose a standout, there is one character who comes to mind when I consider assault survivorship and the tough terrain that exists in navigating its trauma: Margo from Bonnie Jo Campbell's *Once Upon a River*—a novel recently adapted for the screen.

Margo is a complex character, especially where her sexuality is concerned. Although she's a repeat victim of sexual trauma, she also has an active, consensual sex life outside of her assaults.

In a time when victim blaming is rampant, a sexually active gal like Margo doesn't stand a chance when she's assaulted. People, her own family members even, will have different opinions about a girl like *that*. If she's already had sex, it's not like a rape will take anything from her that she hasn't already given away, right? I mean, she likes sex, right? She probably seduced these men, right? Wrong. Wrong. Wrong. No means no. Period. We don't speak this way when we react to other instances when one person violates another person. We don't say, "It's not a big deal so-and-so got beat up because her dad beats her regularly anyway. She's used to it. Probably asked for it." It's not logical to respond this way. Yet this type of reaction is ingrained in our culture's attitudes about sexual contact and where the lines are drawn for consent.

We live in a culture that has popularized the virtuous, upstanding damsel in distress like those Disney princesses. So, when a survivor's reality is more complicated—as with Margo and her active sex life—people often use their flawed moral lens to blame the survivor for her own assault. What I want to emphasize here is that consent is not dictated by a person's sexual history and trauma isn't measured by our previous consensual encounters. Whether you relate to Margo's sexual experience or not, your consent matters. So does your trauma. We're all complex characters who are naturally traumatized by the shock and pain of an assault. It doesn't matter what your sexual ethics are. To be the heroine in your own recovery story, just come dressed as yourself. No need to wear any shame others try to impose on you because of your lifestyle choices or anything that happened to you without your consent.

A CRACK IN THE HOMEFRONT LINE

What if I told you there's a war going on? This war is not waged by power-hungry entities and the armed soldiers they recruit to lay down their lives for the cause. Though a driving force in this war *is* a desire for power and sometimes weapons are involved. The war I reference is so close to home, it might be in your bedroom, outside your front door, in your school or workplace, or on your way to any of these places. It might even be glaring at you from your backlit screen. Maybe the real war is the one raging inside your head—the battleground the places you once found safe, sacred.

Acts of war in this scenario are waged in any variety of abusive or violent actions committed by one person against another in their living environments. While this sounds a lot like domestic violence, these war crimes are not limited to domestic living settings or relationships. The casualties in these wars often do not live with their assailants. Sometimes they don't even know the attacker. There is a phrase I use to label these types of assault situations: **home-front violence**. Home-front violence is defined as the physical and/or mental assaults perpetuated by one person against another in places that make up a person's living environment, including the victim's home, community, and region.

While home-front violence happens to people of all ages and genders, this message is tailored for late teen and new adult girls. If you are a teen or new adult who has experienced home-front violence, you are not alone or without options. The assault that forced a rift in your existence does not need to remain a crack in your foundation.

NOT ANOTHER "DON'T DRINK THE POISON" MESSAGE

You may have heard the expression, "Resentment is like drinking poison and hoping it will kill the other person." Perhaps you just heard this for the first time and you're nodding as you recall all the bitter poison you've swallowed, picturing the justice your assaulter deserves while you relive your attack. I would be lying if I said I never sipped this poison, gulped it like my life depended on it. I have yet to meet a person who hasn't drunk this toxic cocktail. Yet, I've also never met a person who died from ingesting this toxic brew—even those who drink the poison over their lifetime. Instead, what I've seen is how this poison reduces their quality of life in much the same ways a chronic illness would. This said, I don't think readers need another don't-drink-the-poison message. What we need is insight on dead men walking.

DEAD MAN WALKING

Several years ago, I heard a great message about carrying around dead weight. Dead weight is one of those concepts that has become so mainstream, it's lost its graphic luster. For those of you who get squeamish, some of what follows might make you uncomfortable. I hope you will trust and follow me through this section regardless.

Dead weight is an idiom with a long history dating back to ancient times. During the Roman Empire, particularly at its height around AD 100, ancient Roman emperors were known to invent heinous, often bizarre penalties as punishment for crimes. Punishments with weighted items that had a symbolic connection to the crime were a recurrent theme in many of these sentences. This theatrical tactic grew from a long history of punishment playing out as entertainment while promoting social order. Originally, many of these punishments played out in the gladiator arena. When this form of using fear to promote social order became less effective, the accused were forced to walk out their sentences in the streets. This new style of punishment extended the arena and its gladiators into the public sphere where fear could be heightened.

Weight as a symbol for balancing justice traces back centuries to Egyptian Mythology and has been adapted by other cultures since. Tracing back to ancient Egypt, the first goddess of justice is thought to be Ma'at, whose purpose was to balance universal order through truth and law offset by morality and justice (Mark 2016). Fast forward to the Greek goddesses of justice, Themis and her daughter Dike (c. 300 BC), to when the Romans took control of Egypt, and we get Justitia (c. AD 1), the Roman goddess of justice many still refer to today (Gill, 2017). It is not lost on me—and hopefully on you either—that the Romans adopted these weighted punishments from the concept of a blindfolded deity who literally balances the scales. Some of these punishments included forcing a slave to carry a plank of wood on their shoulders or tying a weight to slaves' feet as they were beaten so they, the living merchandise, couldn't flee. Other crimes like treason carried a sentence of being buried alive under the weight of cold, hard earth or drowning after being bound with rocks. But the most gruesome death by weight was reserved for murders. The Romans were known to punish murderers with a life sentence where the dead victim's corpse was strapped to the assassin's bare backside. The murderer was bound to the victim, joined at the wrists, torsos, calves, and ankles for maximum skin-to-skin exposure—sentenced to live while connected to a decaying corpse. Everywhere the murderer went, the victim followed.

Being followed by your victim and haunted by your murderous act will be the least of your concerns. Regardless of how strong—mentally or physically—you feel, the reality of carrying this dead weight soon becomes apparent. Rigor mortis will set in and make movement harder. A few days in, the stench of decay is undeniable and drives others away from you. Soon flies and other pests assist with decomposition. Infectious disease from the decaying corpse slowly enters your body through your skin. Your inevitable death is slow and painful. Death by association is your fate. You were a dead man walking the moment they strapped your victim's dead weight to your back.

Here's what I want you to see, modern reader. All too often, we assume our attacker's punishment. We strap the dead weight of our experience onto our backs and attempt to live a normal, healthy life carrying that rotting corpse as it (literally and figuratively) sucks the life from us. You see, when you carry that dead weight, you become a two-fold victim.

The real solution to your recovery from assault is to cut yourself free from your incident and assailant. The ultimate form of justice occurs when you separate yourself from these things that bind you into cycles of torment. The moment you release that dead weight— this punishment you were never meant to endure—your recovery (and you) will thrive.

LET THE DEAD BURY THE DEAD

Lately, I think a lot about why so many people cling to the details of their assault and assailant. I wonder whether survivors would release the dead weight if they could see how the consequences of holding on hurts them more than they have already been hurt. I wonder all these things because I've lived these experiences and lost some time walking with the dead. Looking back, I wish someone had walked me down a different path toward my recovery—a path free of unintentional self-harm and self-destruction.

Much of my own self-harm and destruction come from being a nonconfrontational person by nature. For me, it was easier to dismiss an incident or conflict than to put all that energy into fighting to be validated, understood, or believed. Better to make myself smaller—invisible even—if it meant avoiding making myself vulnerable to more conflict. Better to shut up before things got heated and no one was left standing next to me. Sound familiar? This is exactly how I lived my teen and young-adult years: as a ghost of myself, haunted by my prior hurts and trapped between the living and the dead. I lost too much time during my teenage years and twenties carrying around the dead weight of my assaults. I carried these burdens as though my identity was tied to them and refused to allow anyone around me to remove or share the load.

It took me years and a whole arsenal of recovery initiatives to break free from focusing on the burdens that were slowly and painfully poisoning my life. When I figured out how to cut myself free from these weighty loads, I felt alive in ways I'd never felt alive before. You're probably wondering what my breakthrough moment was, right? It was realizing I should let the dead bury their dead. In other words, I needed to stop allowing

18

things beyond my control or influence, even things I couldn't change, to distract me from living my life in the here and now. There's more to this, and I promise I'll come back to it in the next chapters.

WAKE ME UP WHEN SEPTEMBER ENDS

Well before Green Day coined the phrase, "Wake me up when September ends," I'd adopted the sentiment as my seasonal motto. I knew this place of intentional slumber. September's been a difficult month for me to get through for as long as I can remember. The culprit: September was the month I was date raped the night before the homecoming dance. It wasn't my first sexual or physical assault, but it was the event that killed what remained of my hope for my future. I became trapped under the weight of what-ifs that came to visit every September.

> *What if we hadn't been under the influence? What if I hadn't worn my favorite mini skirt that night? What if we hadn't gone up to that room to make out? What if my best friend believed me when I told her what happened? What if I refused to go to the dance, even if it meant my friend couldn't go either? What if my parents found out? What if I'd gone to the cops? What if they'd blamed it on me, too? What if I was alone when I passed him in the halls at school? What if I never stopped seeing his cryptic expression when I closed my eyes or the smile he flashed at me over the years when our paths crossed? What if he does it again? Gets away with it again? My God, what if people still blame me for the whole thing? What if . . .*

Not only was I chained to my own dead weight, I was also weighted by things outside my control. Though I entertained these questions all year, September was when I danced with the corpse of what I saw as my biggest failure and took my secret little party to the grave. No one could possibly understand what I felt. No one needed to know my struggle. Smile in place: check. Focus on happy things: check. Stay busy: check. Defer hope: check.

It was only a matter of time before these avoidance attitudes infected other aspects of my life. For the better part of a decade, I walked with my decomposing dreams crumbling and falling away with each step. It's a good thing I left a trail, though. What didn't compost into the ground became a breadcrumb trail that led me back to some of those rotting dreams once I broke free from the dead weight of my assaults.

OVERCOME AN UNJUST WORLD

There's a downed oak at the nature center near my home that reveals the mystery in coming back to life, no matter how far you've fallen or how long you've been down. We originally named it Dead Man Falling. Yet that name doesn't accurately paint the portrait of its existence. The tragic part of this downed tree is that it had to be hundreds of years old before it gave up the good fight and buried its own head in the dirt.

It's unclear how long this tree lay prostrate, its roots loosed from their deep resting place while the earth and life attached to it began growing up around it. This new birth springing forth would be impressive enough if it weren't for the most extraordinary manifestation: row upon row of offspring seedlings and saplings that spanned the entire length of the old beauty. What struck me most the first time I saw this oak's rebirth was how the more mature saplings reached and stretched toward the sun. This was a breakthrough moment for me and a break-free moment in my restoration. Here I stood, my oldest daughter's hand tucked in mine, my middle daughter strapped into my backpack carrier, my youngest asleep in my belly. I looked up toward that same sun, where my life source washed me in a warmth that was a comfort place.

Look how your life has blossomed, the gentle voice within whispered.

Yeah, sure, I thought. *But what if they repeat the cycle? What if my girls have to live through the same things I've gone through?*

Listen to yourself, the voice replied. *Did you not live through these things and thrive despite them? Are you not an overcomer?*

I rolled my eyes. *An overcomer?*

I had been studying and meditating on what it meant to be an overcomer. I'd recently read the word overcomer stemmed from the Greek word *nike*, which means victory in battle. Some of the stuff I read about overcoming this world's battles focused on releasing things to God or the universe. But let me be real with you, reader. I was really struggling with how justice worked in this world and letting go of unresolved things. Though I didn't necessarily *deal with* these unsettled things, I couldn't seem to loosen my grip on them.

As I meditated on what it meant to be an overcomer, I was reminded about the power of conquering fear to regain control of a situation. But living with fear was exactly what I was doing. With each daughter I brought into this unjust world, my what-if list grew, and my fear grew with it.

The gentle voice wasn't done with me yet. *You didn't just move on from the things meant to hurt and destroy you. You conquered them. What you're building will change this narrative.*

And yet I can't forget! No matter how hard I try, I can't forget.

I never told you to forget these things. I told you, the spirit reminded me, *I'd use them to mold you and you'd use them to witness to other survivors.*

My attention was drawn back to the oak in front of us. Oak, extremely durable and strong. Oak, the forest's stable force with enviable endurance. Even knocked to near-death status with no hope of standing tall again in its natural form, it sustained life. And in sustaining its life, it reinvented what that life would look like. Where the tree once stood strong, seven saplings almost as tall as I rose in its place. Seven is a symbolic powerhouse. Seven is the seeker of truth. Seven, the number of completeness. Seven, the number of perfection.

Girl, I thought, squeezing my five-year-old's hand, *there's never been a better time to come back to life.*

unLabeling Things

You may notice I rarely use the word "victim." This is intentional. Though it's accurate to say someone was a victim of assault, to label someone a victim beyond her assault leads to dangerous territory. Labels have power. Labels have long shelf lives. No, really. We literally create labels meant to identify things we store on shelves, cabinets, drawers, and containers. Labels also assign roles and sometimes even become badges we wear to mark these roles.

The word *victim*, by definition, does mean one who has been injured, attacked, wronged, taken advantage of, or killed by violence. It also means one who has been tricked or cheated. Additionally, victims are often portrayed as those who need to be rescued. I avoid using the label victim because I don't want to encourage people to get comfortable in this role or to assume it indefinitely. A label for this is victimhood. Victimhood has evolved into a social class. The term originated to define a person who suffered from a crime, adverse circumstances, or accident. Yet it's modern use is derogatory—playing the "victim card," where the abused fabricates her victimhood to justify or divert her abusive ways, manipulation, or plea for sympathy or attention.

I avoid labels in general because they usually have multiple or underlying meanings that change them into something else. This leads to confusion. Confusion leads to chaos and opens the door for misconception. Confusion is the author of destruction, and there is no space for destruction in the plans I want to share with you. However, I don't want to hinder you label-oriented people from finding good ones if that's what drives you forward. Just consider labels you can live with for a while. Find labels that illustrate you in a position of empowerment as you work toward your recovery and restoration. Consider prophetic labels like survivor, warrior, conqueror, overcomer, victor, perseverer, tenacious one, shieldmaiden, or dragon slayer. Make one up if you can't find a suitable one. Just promise me: if you must choose a label, use one that screams you're the active authority in your assault recovery and restoration. Promise me you'll pick something that reminds you who the hero is in your story: you, the one who will rescue herself. And I promise to show you ways to be your own hero as you rewrite your future narrative. Fair enough?

II
THE ROAD TO RECOVERY

WHEN REINVENTING THE WHEEL HAS YOU CHASING YOUR OWN TAIL

My own recoveries from assault didn't play out exactly as recovery is outlined in this book. This is a major reason I felt led to write this book. Have you ever experienced being totally lost with a new activity, academic interest, job, or sport? Of course you have. We all have. Let me take it a step farther. Have you ever felt lost, struggling to figure out what you need to do next and how you need to do it? Had to figure out how to do something on your own? Have you ever invented your own way of doing things only to have someone say, "You know, there's an easier way to do that. You should've looked up such and such or called so-and-so? Heck, you could've called me had we known each other then!"? And then, after your facepalm moment subsides and your elevated blood pressure regulates, all you want to do is scream, "Why did everyone watch me chase my tail to reinvent a wheel that already existed?" This not only wastes tons of time—it also means you didn't necessarily get everything right or operating optimally because the only tools you used were the ones you guessed or found.

I don't know about you, but I hate this vicious cycle and wonder why some people would rather watch others struggle to figure it out (perhaps like they had to) than share the strategies that allow everyone to achieve success. Here's what I desperately want you to understand: you shouldn't have to reinvent the wheel or give up because you've lost your way. You should also never feel alone when you have a circle of fellow travelers who will willingly gift you the map they charted along their own journey. Just because I didn't benefit from all the recovery initiatives and resources I share with you doesn't mean you shouldn't get to benefit from them. When I imagine the impact of such initiatives on young assault survivors who don't have to carry this dead weight into their adult lives, I can hardly wait to share them with you.

So, pack up that hamster wheel, unfold the map I've placed in your lap, and follow a fellow traveler to restoration and freedom.

WHAT RESEARCH SHOWS AND LACKS

While I don't want to lose you in a full-blown research study analysis, I do want to bring scientific research into this discussion. I've done endless research analysis about assault and assault recovery over the past two decades and want to share some related research that lines up with the outlooks, examples, approaches, and strategies outlined in this book. Trauma recovery isn't a wheel I invented. Rather, it's an ongoing conversation I'm joining and inviting you to join. So, let's dig in.

With every instance of traumatic distress is a potential to work through it and become healed and whole again. There's an intersection where avoidance coping meets confrontation coping that can lead to transformation and empowerment. Avoidance coping is any combination of maladaptive behaviors and attitudes where a survivor tries to avoid or ignore stress triggers rather than deal with them. Confrontation coping is a direct acknowledgement and confrontation of stressful triggers. It's solution-driven and aims to overcome challenges that hinder a survivor from fully engaging in interactions or situations. This intersection growth idea is the premise of the a*RIFT*₊ Warrior Project and this companion book. In the medical world, this growth is called post-traumatic growth (PTG). PTG, which is sometimes called positive life change, happens when an assault survivor experiences improved self-perceptions and confidence, clarity of purpose, and close relationships. This kind of growth is self- and professionally directed. According to research presented in "Posttraumatic Growth Following Sexual Assault" by Patricia A. Frazier and Margit I. Berman (Joseph and Linley 2008), the distress survivors experience after a traumatic assault can potentially be used to initiate positive life changes. This is not to say they promote assault or trauma as good things—just that they can be used by survivors to rebuild themselves. Their research focuses on sexual assault survivors because of their unique post-traumatic stress disorder (PTSD) circumstances and enhanced stigma related to the internal harm caused by their attack. Some of the research literature they cross-examine suggests PTG may be attained quicker by those who pursue it soon after their assault. They also note that survivors reported a more substantial decrease in traumatic distress when PTG occurred through positive life changes. The good news is these decreases in distress and positive life changes were present regardless of how much time had passed since their assault. Frazier and Berman's research findings and literature analysis show a correlation between decreases in distress and improvements in life satisfaction, confidence, spirituality or philosophical views, and improved health perception.

Frazier and Berman's research doesn't present specific strategies survivors can implement as they work toward PTG. In place of specifics, what the available research does offer is assessment of several social and coping factor models. They examine factor models that correlate with social support or lack thereof from ethnic, religious, community, and environmental outlets, as well as individual coping skills and control over the recovery process. In evaluating all these factors, they notice that survivors who take precautions for their current and future safety and control their recovery process show the most self-reported and long-lasting improvements in PTG.

In this book, you'll discover recovery strategies for the self-directed aspects of your recovery process. Many of the strategies outlined later in this book are inspired by trauma-informed therapy initiatives and my own tried and tested techniques, which countless youth and new adults I've mentored have also used with great success. Some of the prompts are the types of homework you could expect your therapist to give you between visits. And although your rehabilitation process will often be self-directed and self-managed, recovering from trauma in total isolation is a difficult task. That's why you'll notice a combination of independent, interactive, and professional options for you to implement as you nurture the relationships that will be crucial to your recovery. I should also reemphasize that it's critical you seek professional help when necessary. There is no shame in this. Only you know the depth of your wounds and ability to cope with them. Your journey to improved quality of life and freedom should be built on an integration of strategies and actions that all intentionally work together for your total healing process.

GRIEVING AIDS RESTORATION

Before we can talk about assault-recovery initiatives, we must confront an often-overlooked consequence of assault: the grief that follows it. At the root of any grief is heartache, the emotional anguish that results from a devastating loss or affliction. We tend to recover from physical distress faster than we do emotional suffering.

When you experience assault-related trauma, avoiding it won't make it go away. Repressing trauma is just that: keeping the feelings under control or hidden. There is a distinct difference between controlling your emotions and resolving them. Eventually, another trigger will force those emotions past your resolve, and your delayed emotional release will likely explode like a forgotten landmine, injuring you and anyone around you in catastrophic ways.

Throughout my youth and young-adult life, I avoided the grieving process. I literally did not grieve. Sure, there were cases when heartache didn't follow trauma. I was, after all, known for such resilience. But my most basic survival technique was to bury grief the moment it surfaced, shoving it into this hollowed out place that made me feel emptier with each addition. I justified this by telling myself I was an ugly crier and crying gave me a headache and swollen eyes for days. I believed I wouldn't be worth a crap to those around me if I let myself fall apart, even for a moment. On top of that, I was afraid making myself more vulnerable than I already was could open me up to more trauma, and I actively avoided conflict because—well, conflict. You can begin to imagine my dysfunction when it came to grief.

When it comes to overcoming grief, confronting it allows your entire healing process to happen quicker. I don't just say this because it sounds good. I say it because I would give anything to go back and reapproach my grief with a recovery mindset. By the time I figured out burying grief didn't kill it and only hindered my total recovery, I felt cheated. Cheated that I prolonged and perpetuated my suffering. Cheated out of living with true peace. Cheated from living my freest, most empowered life. Cheated out of all the time and energy I lost. That's right—you still invest time and energy when you avoid thinking and talking about the emotions you experience from surviving a trauma. Then, you eventually must invest time and energy to work through these emotions when they will no longer stay buried in that internal graveyard. And at that point, these emotions are infected with bitterness and other toxic thoughts that require additional time and attention to resolve. Not to mention how damaging these toxins are to other areas of your life.

Can you imagine if we operated the same way with physical injuries? What would happen if you cut your foot and the only care you offered this wound was the shower you took right after you injured it? Days later, when the pain intensifies and the cut gets infected, you tell yourself to ignore it, you've suffered worse pain. "Mind over matter," you repeat as the wound throbs and itches. Eventually you wake up and notice the pain has diminished. You think the infection worked itself out naturally only to discover a swollen, angry, foul-smelling lesion a few days later. Now you must break down and visit a doctor, who tells you it's turned to gangrene and your foot must be amputated to save your life. Say *what*? We don't rationalize and handle physical injury this way because it's detrimental to our health. Why, then, do so many of us rationalize and handle psychological injury as if ignoring it is how it gets better? Not only does this approach stifle or drastically slow your healing process, but it also affects your daily functions and interactions with others. While you might think your buried emotions don't disturb your outward attitudes, they do. What do you think will happen after your festered toxic bitterness seeps into your relationships? I'll tell you what happens. *You* become the gangrene. People cut you from their lives because no one can chance that stink infecting them, too. You might even begin to irritate yourself.

GRIEF HAS LAYERS

Spoiler alert: not every assault causes emotional trauma and not every emotional trauma causes grief. But because grief *does* rear its ugly head often enough, we need to confront it face-to-face. For those suffering from grief, it feels bleak. Despite the age-old adage, time alone will not relieve grief. Like I mentioned in the previous section, just as physical injuries heal through a process, emotional ones do, too. Physical wound care is structured around a process completed over time, which combines things like procedures, treatments, therapies, and/or prescriptive aids. Rarely is the treatment plan to let time alone do the healing. The same is true for emotional wounds.

Although the healing process for emotional wounds differs from physical ones, it's still just as important to optimizing quality of life. Emotional recovery focuses more on healing stages than on procedures, treatments, therapies, and/or prescriptive aids. Though some healing stages will benefit from these options. If we look close enough, we'll notice recovery for the two injury types has more in common than we realized.

To deal with grief, it's first important to understand the patterns in which it manifests. Most grief frameworks have evolved from psychiatrist Elisabeth *Kübler-Ross's* five stages of grief (which she later revised to include seven stages): shock, denial, anger, bargaining, depression, testing, and acceptance. Through my research, training, and experience, I've adapted an eight-stage list that hits the major areas assault victims typically experience. These stages are shock and denial, pain, recall, guilt and shame, anger, depression, acceptance and hope, and recovery. Don't get caught up in the order or whether you've experienced every stage. A person can experience all or any of these stages in any sequence and can even repeat stages multiple times. You can even experience more than one stage at the same time. Also, when grieving a physical or sexual assault, you may have to deal with physical and emotional healing simultaneously. The bottom line: grief patterns are unique for each person.

If you're someone who has experienced grief without relief after an assault or are now waist-high in a grief experience and sinking, what follows is for you.

STAGES OF ASSAULT GRIEF

1. Shock & Denial

One of the initial sensations during an assault and immediately following it is shock. Shock can impact a grief process during other stages, but its role in these initial instances is most common. Shock is a survival mechanism as much as it's a logical reaction to being caught off guard by an attack. Numbness, disbelief, uncanny calmness, and confusion are natural psychological responses to trauma caused by violence. Conversely, mental numbness and brain fog are subconscious strategies we sometimes invoke during a traumatic experience to mentally separate ourselves from the assault and our attacker. Shock can also impact physical conditions and reactions.

Because of these instinctive reactions to assault, shock usually fades into denial, a coping skill that only allows so much detail in at a time. Denial consists of those impressions that tell you what's happening to you isn't real, can't possibly be real. *No, no, no,* you rationalize, *these horrific things only happen to other people. Why me? I swore I'd never allow this to happen to me.* Denial often happens later, in the heat of an assault or immediately following it. *Is this really happening? Did that just happen or am I recalling a scene from a horror film I saw? Am I remembering things right?* The struggle here is that shock and denial often make us question our own reality. To deny the incident and your feelings about it also means you choose to reject them as your truth.

Shock and denial comprise a coping strategy that protects you from dealing with too much so you can simply survive another moment or another day. Therefore, time-lapsed shock and denial often creep into other stages of grief. Numbness from shock can fog your entire grief process. The world as you know it might not make sense as you walk through this hazy reality. From this disadvantaged perspective, you may even question if it's possible or worth it to get through this. Denial kicks in so you're not overwhelmed with all your emotions at once.

2. Pain

Pain is a vague word that works better as a tag or place marker. The word pain can describe any type of sensory or psychological suffering or discomfort. Any good editor will flag the word pain and say to use specific language. Why say great pain when agony, torture, torment, trauma, wound, burn, sting, spasm, throb, misery, distress, anguish, or heartache evoke a more specific suffering? Such specificity is an important factor when addressing your pain areas. To keep things simple, I'll use the word pain here as a general reference.

Whether pain is experienced during an attack or after it, it's not wise to ignore it or pretend it doesn't exist. Trust me when I say I know how hard it is to confront and deal with physical *and* emotional pain caused by an assault. But pain is a trigger warning you shouldn't ignore. Pain is the body's or mind's way of getting your attention so you can address an issue. If, for instance, you experience physical pain during an assault and this pain persists afterward, it's important to assess and treat the pain so whatever is causing it doesn't progress into something worse. The same is true for emotional pain. Any emotional pain you experience during and after an attack should be assessed and treated. How you choose to treat physical and emotional pain is entirely up to you. Whether a medical professional prescribes medication, treatment, and rest or your prior experience leads you to other treatment options, these are still pain management plans. Whether you work with a counselor, therapist, or trusted friend to develop emotional treatment strategies or figure out your own plan after time alone with your journal, it still leads you to a pain management plan.

It's important we distinguish a few things about healthful versus non healthful pain management. First, self-medicating through alcohol and substances are not what I mean by self-guided treatment options. These are temporary escapes that have no positive impact on your healing and long-term goals. Relying on substances should be your first clue about how harmful these are to your recovery process. Second, there are times medical intervention is necessary—and that's OK. Refusing to acknowledge that you need help is a clear case of denial, which cycles you back to that first grief stage. Sometimes it's hard to know when to use professional and self-care options. If you ever feel like things are just too much or you're stuck in your healing process, these might be clues you need help beyond yourself and existing support circle. If you're a teen who doesn't have supportive parents or guardians, or you don't have good health insurance, it may be hard to find help. You can find some help options in the next section under "Professionally Guided Versus Self-Guided Treatment Options" and at www.aRIFTwarriorproject.org/services-resources. Whatever options you use, promise yourself you will choose care that meets your needs. Using escape methods and refusing the right help when you need it are forms of self-harm, which hurt you more than you've already been hurt. More hurt causes more pain, which is counterintuitive, right?

3. Recall

Recall happens when you remember the details of your assault and relive the trauma. There is a lot of research out there about the human brain's instinct to mentally relive traumatic experiences. A main reason our brains operate this way is because it's natural to seek the logic from experience. Remembering allows us to examine the details of an incident and the reasoning behind it. Humans are inclined to make sense of and learn from traumatic experiences for many reasons, including not wanting to repeat them. It's both natural and healthy to evaluate an unpleasant experience so we can reveal the context of our trauma, the levels of loss, what these mean in our life, and what role, *if any*, we played. Our healing often relies on uncovering and understanding these aspects of our experience. However, recalling can also trap you in a place that is more harmful than good.

After my middle daughter was physically attacked in high school—an incident where she was sucker punched from behind and didn't defend herself for fear of punishment—I did what any modern mama does with the emergency room diagnosis: I learned everything I could about assault and battery recovery. What was most surprising about my findings were the PTSD-like symptoms these assault victims experience because of constant recall of their attack. Like many of the PTSD patients I've read about or coached over the years, assault survivors tend to recall their trauma often and daily, whether awake or asleep. Constantly recalling trauma causes them to relive the pain and hopelessness they experienced. This also perpetuates rather than diminishes everyday triggers that set off their stress reactions and fuel anxiety. It's such a dangerous cycle that some experts in PTSD therapy challenge traditional therapy approaches like prolonged exposure (PE), which forces patients to relive trauma for the sake of desensitizing them (van der Kolk, McFarlane, and Weisaeth 2007). I see this strategy as detrimental to recovery because it does nothing to help survivors learn and heal from their traumatic encounter.

The challenge to navigating the recall stage is to distinguish between what leads to self-help and self-harm. It's healthy to seek to understand and learn from trauma so we can make peace with and heal from it. However, it's dangerous to torment ourselves until we desensitize our reaction to our violent encounter. How long do you suppose it would take to become nonreactive to your own trauma? How do you suppose developing indifference to violence committed against you will affect your self-respect and future? Do you see future incidents as irrelevant because you are numb to your exposure to violence? Will this influence how you see and react to violence other people endure? The million-dollar question here is this: is your desensitized state situational, or is it one giant leap into a lifetime of larger psychological problems?

You won't necessarily recall details in order and you won't know what will trigger a memory until it happens. Memories contain pockets and wrinkles: some aren't meant to be emptied or smoothed out, and others will fall into place with the right attention. Think of recall as a sifting process that might occur on an archeological dig. Recall is meant to help you process the effects of the memory, not torture yourself. You are looking for details that will help make sense of your trauma and its impact on you. These are the details that help make meaning out of your trauma, as well as its triggers and impacts on all areas of your life. Believe it or not, by figuring out these triggers, you can reduce anxiety, depression, and hopelessness and begin to heal.

You'll likely recall painful details from your assault without respect for if or how it will aid your grieving process. This is the unfortunate nature of traumatic memory recall. In these instances, it's helpful to confront these memories and put them in check so they don't distract your efforts to restore your emotional health. Sometimes it can become difficult to check destructive memories or independently work through memory details. In these instances, you might not be ready to channel into those parts of the memory. It's okay to stop a recall exercise in such cases and maybe just note which memory details you hope to focus on next time you try. It may take some practice, but it's possible to redirect your focus when it gets off track. For instance, when your thoughts keep taking you back to graphic details of your assault, remind yourself you're only interested in the emotional and/or physical impacts it had on you or [fill in the blank] with your specific mission. Some other strategies to try are outlined in **Part III**, under the section **Day 7 is Rest-and-Recharge Day**.

Don't delay using outside support and treatment options if you experience significant or persistent issues when you cannot shut down harmful thoughts or memories. These could be instances when you just can't stop recalling the graphic details or, in trying to work through recall, you uncover other memories that trigger new trauma that you feel like you can't deal with on your own. Remember that distinction I made earlier about self-help versus self-harm? Well, significant or persistent problems are clear signs it's time for external support. Getting the right support early on is a vital, proactive approach to regaining your best quality of life. Outside support and treatment might come in the form of seeing a counselor, therapist, or doctor. In some instances, medications may be beneficial in addition to counseling and therapies. Find support options and resources in **Part III** under **Professionally Guided Versus Self-Guided Treatment Options** and at www.aRIFTwarriorproject. org/services-resources.

4. Guilt & Shame

Next on the list is guilt and shame. Guilt and shame is a tough stage to discuss because there are vast reasons and triggers for these emotions. Any way you view it, guilt and shame are negative emotions that undermine a person's grief progress. While guilt and shame are closely linked concepts, they aren't interchangeable words. Guilt stems from the root cause of an offense or negative instance. Guilt fills you with remorse and leaves you feeling responsible for doing something wrong, whether you contributed to the wrongdoing or not. While shame is a consequence of or an emotional reaction to a wrongdoing and it also isn't always about playing a part in the instance. Shame acts like an internal mirror that reflects the bad way you feel about yourself and how this reflection may be viewed by others.

Hindsight can't transport you back in time to change the course of events just as beating yourself up for not seeing or doing things to prevent your attack can't alter the past. Let me also point out an irony in this line of thinking. The meaning of the word attack originates from a plan to defeat an enemy by force. This is war language. Attack strategies are meant for war, not civilian life. We are not at war in our communities. We should therefore not have to act and prepare like we are or feel like failures when we fall victim to an attack because another person went rogue against human decency. Think about that for a moment before moving on.

The guilt and shame trigger list is endless and includes thoughts like:

- Why didn't I do anything or more to stop my attack?
- Did I deserve or provoke what happened to me?
- Maybe if I hadn't done, worn, or said . . .
- Maybe I should've taken this to the grave so people didn't pity or judge me.

- I hate that my trauma causes other people so much pain.
- Is it wrong to hope for my attacker's suffering? For justice? Vengeance?
- How can anyone love or want me now?
- What will people think of me now?
- Will I always feel this powerless over my life?
- Am I overacting? Handling things fairly? Reasonably?
- Do I really wear my victimhood like a badge of honor?
- Should I still be struggling to get past this?
- Should I still feel this powerless? Hopeless? Resentful?
- Shouldn't we all focus on more important things?
- Worse things have happened to better people.
- I'm dwelling, I know I am. No one takes this long to move on.

I'll stop here. You get the picture, and it's not a pretty one. Guilt and shame can hinder your healing if you don't work through your list and the regret at the root of these reactions. Regardless of what your brain says you could or should have done differently, your attacker is wholly responsible for your assault. Period. Anytime you try to find responsibility for provoking your attack, tell yourself, "I'm not responsible for my assault and I don't share any of my attacker's guilt." To entertain any other thought perpetuates a futile, vicious cycle.

When it comes to working through the guilt and shame process, choose the proactive route that brings closure. Expose what you need to expose so you can identify and work through your emotions and realign them with truth. Work through all these negative emotions until you free their hold on and influence over you. Then, when guilt and shame rear their ugly heads again, speak against them with the power, authority, and truth you gained during your first run-in with these beasts.

5. Anger

Anger is another one of those vague words that an editor would flag for revision. Anger can mean anything. Anger can mean annoyed, displeased, hostile, furious, vexed, pissed, irritated, enraged, outraged, aggravated, resentful, exasperated, and provoked. Each one of these words has a distinctly different meaning and association, which tells us a little more about what's going on emotionally. Anger, then, becomes a category we use when discussing strong feelings and reactions we have to traumatic stimuli. Identifying and dealing with specific anger emotions that result from your assault are necessary and helpful parts of the grief process.

Most of us can agree on a few things when it comes to anger. Anger knows no limits. It's an automatic response to pain. Anger is an earned emotion for assault survivors. It's natural to be angry with the person who hurt you. It's also natural to be angry about being forced to endure your attack. Sometimes anger is the only rational emotion you have about your attack and attacker when all your other emotions are all over the place. Though anger is a normal and sometimes healthy emotion, it can quickly turn destructive. Anger, when suppressed, can make you explosive. Anger has a caustic effect on emotions, which impacts a person's mental *and* physical health. Because anger covers other emotions like fear, anxiety, pain, guilt, shame, and depression, it often weaves itself in and out of the other grief stages.

We typically respond to anger by suppressing, expressing, easing, or teasing it. How you respond while angry determines if this portion of your grief process will produce positive, productive results or negative setbacks. When not confronted, anger can infect other areas in your life and lead to problems that reduce your total quality of life. When not managed, it can lead to chronic irritability or aggression, where anger becomes a default response for every emotional trigger. Since anger is a normal and healthy response to trauma, finding healthy ways to express it promotes emotional healing. I wish I had the formula for the optimal healthy response to anger, but it doesn't exist. I can, however, offer you a few effective strategies for teasing out, expressing, and easing anger.

Agency and self-control are at the forefront of my list. Own your anger and root your expression of it to your values. In other words, don't lose yourself in your outward expression of your inward suffering. Let your anger redirect you toward solutions to issues or struggles you experience after your assault. Allow your anger to tease out the things that have and continue to hurt you so you can communicate them, get support for them, and change their hold on you. Find healthy mental and physical outlets for your anger. Journal, meditate, or pray on what you can do to work through the anger. Talk to someone you trust about your anger. Find a physical activity or exercise. And don't stop here. Implement strategies that have worked for you in the past and find new ones that help you release or ease your anger in proactive ways.

Ultimately, triggered anger should motivate positive action. It should allow you to deflect your focus from your suffering so you can identify, cope with, and resolve the emotional damages from your assault. Remember, an anger release is a good thing. It promotes emotional recovery and can even give you a shot of confidence that empowers you to reclaim control over your emotions. You can even use anger to convert vulnerable or helpless feelings into reclaimed power and control over your life. Every step you take to identify, release, and manage your anger proactively is a step closer to your assault recovery and restoration.

6. Depression

Depression, anger's hangover. Anger is the sugar high for which depression is that inevitable sugar crash. These two stages are often back-to-back for this reason. What energy we draw in a fit of rage will usually fade into lethargy, where we move in slow motion through some darkened dreamscape that vaguely resembles the world we know. Depression will find you at your most vulnerable. That moment you feel totally alone, worthless, and nothing, and I mean nothing, makes you feel better, is when you know depression—that unwelcome house guest—has arrived. Depression creeps in when the full magnitude of your sadness wrecks your sleep and thought patterns until hopelessness fogs your everyday interactions. Depression hits when you struggle to make peace with your traumatic experience and your coping skills are beyond overwhelmed. Meanwhile, the whole time your depression is with you, it saps your motivation to deal with it.

Depression may be situational or clinical in nature. The depression we'll discuss in this grief stage is situational—the despair and hopelessness caused by your assault and your journey to cope with and move forward from it. Situational depression should not be interchanged with clinical depression, though clinical depression is typically affected by it. If you're already on a treatment plan with a professional, it's important to consult this expert when you incorporate other treatment strategies into your existing plan.

Most assault survivors experience some level of situational depression at least once during their grieving process. This short-term depression is activated after the traumatic incident or stress-related changes experienced in its aftermath. Don't be shocked if depression hits you right around that time everyone around you begins to think you've gotten over your assault grief. They've watched you get mad and blow up about your trauma, right? So, naturally that should mean you got it all out of your system, right? It's normal after an assault to experience depression caused by fear, despair, sorrow, anguish, and hopelessness. It's normal to cry, feel lost or worthless, isolate yourself, and not want to hear one more concerned person tell you how to pull yourself out of it. Often, time alone with your sorrow so you can reflect on your emotions is exactly what you need to move through this stage. But it's also just as normal to seek support from others who've recovered from assault or experts who are trained in this area. A good support circle can offer understanding and insight when you need it most. Always seek help if you experience suicidal thoughts or if your depression intensifies over time.

There's a BUT part of this stage we can't ignore. Situational depression won't just blow over if you ignore it or distract yourself long enough. The whole reason it's considered a short-term issue is because you WORK through the emotions. When you work through situational depression from an assault, you're doing some important things. You're mourning a violent act committed against you. You're defragmenting the distress that hinders your healing. You're learning and implementing new coping skills. You're realigning your self-worth and confidence as you recognize your attack does not define you. You're preparing to move forward from your assault without dismissing its effect on you. That's right—no one gets to tell you your assault didn't affect you or dismiss the tidal wave of emotions that have flooded your thoughts since. For every cause and effect there is a consequence. Or, as I like to say, there are multiple effects and consequences that result from one violent act (cause). If you approach this like a problem that must be solved, it will make sense to invest time in finding and applying a solution. Any way you view it, promise me, yourself, and everyone who cares about you that you will use this time to work through your emotions. And, if you're having a tough time doing this, make sure to seek professional help so you're not stuck in this stage long-term or worse—indefinitely. The world is a better place with you functioning well within it. I promise that it does get better as you work through these grief stages.

7. Acceptance & Hope

Before we discuss what this next stage is, let me premise one important distinction up front. Acceptance does not mean you are finally okay with what happened to you. Acceptance means you've reached a state of peace despite what happened to you. Anyone who tells you that you should reach a point where you're okay about your assault doesn't know what they're talking about. Why should you ever feel okay being physically and/or sexually assaulted? That's a ridiculous notion—one which I heard too many times during my own assault recoveries. No, the acceptance to which I refer is that internal place of peace where hope for an untethered future reigns supreme.

Along these same lines, let's take a moment to break down a mainstream misconception about acceptance from a faith perspective. Whether you're a spiritual person or not, I think everyone can appreciate the concepts in this paragraph. We often hear phrases thrown around when bad things happen that suggest we should just accept our fated lot as it was assigned. What absolute nonsense. Such ill-informed logic, reasoning, and theology lead to the worst, most insensitive advice. Nowhere in biblical scripture does it say, "Everything happens for a reason." No way! Stop telling people who have experienced something traumatic to accept it as God's or the universe's predesigned plan for their life of suffering. The truth is horrible things happen to good people who don't deserve to get caught up in someone else's evil actions.

What scripture does say is that God will use our horrible experiences to bring something good out of them. Do you see the difference? God is not the author of evil: He is the editor who rewrites the outcome for your benefit.

So, what exactly happens at the acceptance and hope stage? Well, for starters, the acceptance stage is a survivor's concession to the reality of her situation and its impact on her. It's birthed from a place of understanding that opens the way for readjustment in all areas of your physical and psychological worlds. While you can never change what happened to you, you can (re)learn to live fully again despite it. Acceptance, then, becomes a belief that from this moment forward—regardless of justice, apology, or remorse—your hope is fixed on a better future.

This is where hope becomes most impactful. Hope is what prepares you to enter the recovery stage. Without hope, there is no confident expectation that positive things are to come. Hope is restorative and allows you to dream again about your best possible future. Through hope, you begin to believe in your goals and dreams, which motivates you to take those initial steps back into the land of the living. Your hope is as strong as your desire for this future you imagine.

You may be powerless to change the awful things that happened to you in the past. However, you do get to choose how you grow or regress from your suffering. Some people call this resilience. But the most important thing is not how quickly you bounce back into a shape that resembles your former self but rather that you find your way to a place where hope fills you with confident expectation for a reclaimed quality of life.

8. Recovery

Whereas all the other stages in some way revolve around your assault, recovery is when your daily focus no longer centers on it. Perhaps it will look something like this: you wake up one day and the fog you've lived in begins to lift. You realize the burden you've carried in this haze is dead weight. When you cut yourself free from this repressive load, you must relearn how to function without that extra weight.

There is nothing as sweet as returning to a healthy state of physical and mental strength after enduring a difficult period. Recovery: a healing process that rehabilitates, reclaims, recaptures, regains, repossesses, recoups, and retakes. Repeat all those defining terms again, slower this time. Notice their essence is each rooted in empowerment, in taking back control and putting back on track. I don't know about you, but I draw so much encouragement from these defining traits of the recovery process. I take back my opening statement: there is nothing as sweet as reclaiming control over your life and circumstances. Second to that is reclaiming your health.

Assault, by its very nature, causes bilateral trauma. Any type of assault requires physical contact, which will have some degree of physical consequences. In addition, being overpowered and battered shock the psyche. As a result, your recovery will require varying degrees of physical and psychologic healing. Anyone who has rehabilitated after any type of physical or psychological injury will confess how difficult the journey is, how much of a personal commitment is involved, and how there is no definite timeframe for making a full recovery. Yet, anyone who has gone through recovery will tell you the journey is worth it. It could take days, weeks, months, even years before you recover from your assault trauma. There is also no guarantee you will make a full recovery. Every recovery situation is different, as are the individuals who must work through them. Rather than focus on a perfect formula, focus on establishing a recovery plan and trying a variety of strategies and/or treatments. The section Assault-Recovery Initiatives in the next chapter gets into specific strategies and treatments to consider in your recovery plan.

III
WELCOME TO THE
VALLEY OF RESTORATION

FROM THE SWEAT OF YOUR BROW COMES SUCCESS

Now that you're more familiar with assault trauma grief stages and why it's important to work through them, you're ready for what follows: the actual work it takes to recover so you can finally live again, free of your trauma's burden. I hope you discover many smart ways within these pages to promote your emotional recovery that lighten your workload. And remember, the rewards come through the personal risks you take in your recovery and restoration journey.

A lot of my recovery resilience is connected to my spiritual life. If you're not a spiritual person, that's okay because this isn't about to dive into a spiritual message or salvation call. If you're looking for that, though, there are plenty of other books out there that serve this purpose. I want to mention the faith-inspired aspects of recovery because they inform some core strategies in the challenges section and are also misunderstood by people from all walks of life. I operate by faith in all areas of my life. Recovery is no exception. At its core, spiritual faith is placing your hope in the promise of things to come. What drives this hope is faith in, of, and from a higher power that is rooted to the belief that there is a way out of every situation where you emerge the victor. This way out is usually accomplished through guided steps and processes where you—the one hoping to be victor at the end of your story—are an active participant in completing these things. Don't expect some lightning bolt to strike down and miraculously shock you with your full recovery. Though miracles do happen, none of us would be reading this page right now if our recovery had already been supernaturally handed down to us. I've worked through my own recoveries with my own sweat and resources I've been led to or given, heavenly or earthly. And I'm okay with this reality because this work ethic and outlook have shaped my character and inform all areas of my life. When you work for your own personal success, victory is never sweeter.

It surprises me how many people I've crossed paths with who live by the notion that they will give their burden to God or a therapist or a trusted confidant who will work it all out for them. Things don't get resolved this way. Seeking help is just that—assistance in some form. This reminds me of a parable about a man who operates this way, and it costs him his life. Perhaps you've heard it before. Here's my version of the story. There's a man who gets swept up in a flood. He manages to grab onto a tree to stop himself from getting carried off to his death. He prays, "God, save me." Within minutes, he hears a loud clunk on the other side of the trunk he holds for dear life. He's able to grab the object and pull it around. It's a kayak. He always loved to kayak, he thinks, releasing the boat to the current. Shortly after, two guys in a rowboat approach and ask if the man needs help. "Thanks," he replies, "but help is on the way." The men nod and row away. The man begins to shiver. An hour passes before a helicopter hovers overhead. "Hey," an air rescue ranger shouts as he slides down a rope. He lowers a tethered harness toward the man. "Slip your arms through this and fasten it around your waist," he says. "No thanks," the stranded man replies. "Help is on the way." The perplexed ranger flips a thumbs up to the pilot and they fly away. Eventually the guy can't hold on any longer. He drowns in the floodwaters that carry him away. When he gets to heaven he says to God, "Why didn't you save me? I prayed and prayed and You never came." God shakes His head. "I tried to save you. I left a tree standing in your path so you could pull yourself to safety. I ensured its branches were low enough for you to climb out of the water until the storm calmed. When you didn't help yourself up the tree, I sent the kayak, which you surrendered to the current. So, I sent the men in the rowboat, which you turned away. As a last attempt, I had my best guys offer to airlift you to safety, but you refused the helicopter's help." The man is bewildered. "That was You the whole time?" he says. "Yes, I was in all of that. But even I can't help you if you won't help yourself."

Here's the thing, fellow traveler. No matter what methods, strategies, and/or assistance you consider, none of them will help with your recovery if you don't do your part. Every ounce of progress you make on your recovery journey will come from the sweat of your own brow. Every strategy, process, or resource will require you to take a step to work through that particular trauma point. Even a prescription will require you to take a specific dose at fixed times. The medication won't do a dang thing to treat your symptoms if it remains in the bottle on your nightstand. Nor will it work properly if you don't take the prescribed dose as stated. You must do the work to complete each step in your recovery. Sadly, no one can walk this leg of your journey for you. Even though life sometimes throws you into these traumatic situations, you have what it takes to be your own hero and save your own lost world. Inside each of you is that Alita warrior spirit. There has never been a better time than right now to come back to life—to reclaim your power, restore your identity, and recover your world. Everything you need to begin is right here. Warrior sister, are you ready to be the hero and reclaim your rightful place in your own life?

DETOUR AHEAD: ALTERNATE ROUTE ADVISED

After an assault, many survivors may have to weigh their options regarding whether to pursue legal/civil justice or not. That's why it's important to know your options and rights. More specifically, it's important to know you have options, protections, and recourse. Maybe your physical assault roughed you up a little or maybe it battered the crap out of you. Maybe your sexual assault left no visible signs or maybe it radically wrecked your body as it did your mind. If your story is anything like mine, it's even possible you belong to the frequent survivor club. My abusive background conditioned me to believe I had no options or recourse. Then, assault after assault reaffirmed my sense of helplessness and resolve that this was just the way these things worked. You know that fight or flight response analogy? Well, my response to crisis used to be a third option: freeze. I share this because these are all common responses and can each lead us down a destructive road.

Take the fight reaction, for instance. Fighting back during an attack can sometimes be effective in stopping or minimizing your assault, just as fighting back afterward can sometimes bring justice against your attacker or offer you necessary protections. But the desire to fight can also evoke ideas of revenge. If you so desire, seek justice not revenge. Don't plot or act out a revenge scheme to harm the person who harmed you. This only opens you up to further harm and can even carry criminal consequences. Though justice isn't served to every deserving assailant and revenge isn't a proactive way of serving it, I've seen the universe serve some villains with its own vengeance.

My favorite instance of this happened back when I was in high school. The first part of the story is my assault experience—my least favorite part—at the hands of a male upperclassman. Two days before state playoffs, the quarterback physically assaulted me in our crowded senior hall. No one, including a teacher passing by, stopped the attack. It was, after all, two days before the biggest game of the year for our defending league champs. Those football players were invincible, and they knew it. I would soon learn this when the school found a loophole in properly addressing and punishing the incident.

You're probably wondering what provoked this attack, right? It turned out some kids were rehashing an old incident where this guy had cheated on his now girlfriend with his ex-girlfriend. Which, I should add, was the girlfriend he cheated on with his now girlfriend. You with me still? Sometimes it's hard to keep your girls straight, but I digress. Anyway, my name came up because I was at a party where he got caught cheating. This was old news, and while I was not the reason he was exposed, hearing my name riled him up. He raced to find me at my locker after this class, his girlfriend pleading at his heels. My friend, who was the girl who tossed my name into that gossip session, said, "I didn't mean to drag you into this," just before my head was slammed into my locker. Strong hands grabbed my shoulders and spun me around so we were face-to-face. This jerk shoved me again and again into that locker. The lock and lever stabbed between my shoulder blades. Each time I bounced back, he shoved harder. The whole time, he spat derogatory names at my face and accusations about how nosy I was. He even said he was going to kill me. His girlfriend begged him to stop, but he pushed her aside each time she touched his arm. My downcast eyes were on his groin, but I couldn't force my knee to do what my mind envisioned. When the bell rang, everyone cleared that hall but me. I fled the school and sought comfort from my boyfriend, who hit the neighborhood with revenge plans of his own. Thankfully, he never found my attacker that night.

Fast forward to summer. I was tight with a group of guys who treated me like a sister whenever we hung out. I loved these guys like the brothers I never had, and I envied their outward strength, their fearlessness in using it. I never had to worry about guys even approaching me when we were out together, which could get frustrating, but I always knew I was safe. Some of us lost contact when they graduated and went off to college, the military, or full-time jobs. But lost contact didn't break the unspoken oath they had to protect me. My best friend at the time, another guy from this group, called me up one day with a scoop he couldn't wait to share with me. He told me how our friend had shown up to a party and noticed my attacker's classic Corvette parked out front. The friend told a few other party guests who also just showed up to tell the jerk to get outside. Then he started busting up things on the car until said jerk came running out in a panic. This clown had no idea why his car was getting a beating, nor why the beating turned to him when he tried to stop our friend. Our friend waited until they were surrounded by bystanders to clue this jerk in on why he'd just gotten his butt kicked. When this jerk was crying and pleading for him to stop, our friend said, "That's for beating up a girl. Don't ever touch my friends again."

My point in sharing this is not to glorify this outcome. Rather, it's to demonstrate how justice has a way of working itself out sometimes, even when we don't pursue it ourselves. You see, I had forgiven the assault already so I could find peace and move forward from it. This forgiveness was for me. It didn't mean I trusted this guy or that he was released from the consequences of his actions against me. Consequences catch up with a person, regardless of which form of justice they take. Even if traditional justice is delivered exactly as the law says it should be, it isn't always served in ways we want—and this is if we even want to pursue it at all. Our systems are unfortunately complicated this way. When my friend told me this story, I initially felt bad. I never asked for anyone to vandalize that jerk's car or rough him up. The only thing that felt good was that a fellow friend was so outraged by my assault, he wanted to restore my honor the only way he knew how. My best friend laughed when I mentioned I didn't take pleasure in this. He told me I was missing the point. "The irony here is that guys like him always get what's coming to them," he said. "It might take some time, but it always catches up with them." I couldn't argue with that. "But why the car?" I asked. "Because he respects his car more than he does people," he replied. "Think of it this way: smashing up the car was equivalent to roughing up his girl. That probably hurt his pride the most."

I didn't have to do one thing to set this outcome in motion because my attacker did the moment he shoved my face into that locker. Yet, too many attackers don't get the justice or punishment they deserve. Or you don't get to see it served when it eventually comes their way. The world is an unfair place in this regard. However, your growth and healing can occur regardless.

RECOVERY STARTS HERE

For too long, physical and sexual assault was normalized for young women—a kind of coming-of-age experience. But assault is still assault, regardless of how you label it. Finally, we live in a time when people are calling out these abuses for the atrocities they are. This new outlook is an anthem catching wind in our nation. Predatory assailants seem to be exposed almost daily. As these winds shift, more and more survivors are surfacing, and the collective emotional turbulence is unsettling. Some are in the heat of recovering from a recent assault. Others are forced to relive past encounters when fellow survivors break the long silence. Whatever your own situation and timeline, your recovery begins when you initiate it.

Repeat after me: **I am not defined by my assault**(s). I want you to keep one more truth in mind as you move forward in these next pages. You are NOT ruined by your assault. Damaged, maybe. But not ruined. As much as you might wish, you can't erase what happened to you. You can, however, rewrite how your story ends.

Assault of any kind is a violation of your body and a theft of your power to protect it. Just as there are no two identical assaults, neither are there two same survival experiences. For this reason, it's impossible to propose one formula that survivors should follow to recover from trauma they experience during and after their attack. This section will outline several recovery initiatives and resources you can implement in your recovery plan. Additional recovery strategies and resources are available and updated regularly at aRIFTwarriorproject.org.

PROFESSIONALLY GUIDED VERSUS SELF-GUIDED
TREATMENT OPTIONS

I like to share the professional resources and outreach options up front so they're easiest to find in this section, especially in moments of crisis. There are way more professional options and assault support venues available than I can possibly list here. Those listed have trusted reputations and/or offer resources that best fit the assault-recovery objectives outlined in this book. For a growing list, visit aRIFTwarriorproject.org.

You may require professional options for legal, medical, and necessary support matters. It's important to find the right support, and the earlier you do it, the better. Here are some options that will help you learn your victim rights and what legal options are available if you seek justice, financial support, or protections. Included here are also crisis intervention helplines, other assault-recovery outreach, and intervention treatment options.

Professional Crisis Resources, Agencies, and Related Outreaches

- National Sexual Assault Helpline
  (800) 656-HOPE (4673) or Online Chat for Help hotline.rainn.org/online

- Crisis Text Line
  Text HOME to 741741, www.crisistextline.org/

- RAINN (Rape, Abuse & Incest National Network)
  (800) 656-4673 | www.rainn.org/recovering-sexual-violence

- National Center for Victims of Crime
  (202) 467-8700 | victimsofcrime.org/help-for-crime-victims/get-help-bulletins-for-crime-victims/trauma-of-victimization

- Sutter Health Palo Alto Medical Foundation Trauma Self-Help
  www.pamf.org/teen/life/trauma/

- National Suicide Prevention Lifeline
  (800) 273-TALK (8255)
  suicidepreventionlifeline.org/

- Project Semicolon Teens
  projectsemicolon.com/ps-teens/project-semicolon-teens/

- National Alliance on Mental Illness
  (800) 950-6264, https://www.nami.org/findsupport/nami-helpline

- Health Center Program, low to no cost primary and preventative health care providers for under insured and uninsured patients: https://findahealthcenter.hrsa.gov/

Law Enforcement, Government and Legal Agencies

- U.S. Department of Education's Office of Civil Rights (OCR)
  (800) 421-3481 | www2.ed.gov/ocr

- National Women's Law Center
  (202) 588-5180 | www.nwlc.org

- American Association of University Women
  (800) 326-AAUW (2289) | www.aauw.org

- American Civil Liberties Union (ACLU)
  Know your rights under Title IX www.aclu.org/title-ix-and-sex-ual-violence-schools

- Equal Rights Advocates—Fighting for Women's Equality
  www.equalrights.org/legal-help/know-your-rights/sexual-ha-rassment-at-school/

Medical Intervention Treatment and Group Therapy Options

- Psychoeducational groups and therapy:

- Cognitive Behavioral Intervention Therapy (CBT)
  A psychotherapeutic therapy that helps survivors identify and understand thoughts and emotions that influence behaviors associated with their trauma (*Journal of Interpersonal Violence*).

- Cognitive Processing Therapy (CPT)
  A cognitive behavioral intervention therapy that is specifically targeted for PTSD recovery (Psychology Today, n.d.).

- Acceptance and Commitment Therapy approach (ACT)
  A type of group therapy inspired by CBT, where mental health professionals teach specialized coping strategies to members with a similar assault diagnosis so clients can share struggles and concerns as they learn (TheraPlatform, n.d.).

- Prolonged-Exposure Therapy (PET)
  A form of psychotherapy developed by Edna Foa, PhD, which helps clients work through unwanted thoughts, depression, helplessness, recurrent nightmares, and other trauma triggers so they can gradually reengage in all aspects of life (Psychology Today, n.d.).

- Eye-Movement Desensitization Reprocessing (EMDR)
  A treatment created by Francine Shapiro based on adaptive information processing, which is designed to help survivors heal from dysfunctional memory bits that cause emotional trauma so they can approach present and future situations with cautious composure and flexibility (Psychology Today, n.d.).

- Connect with a local support group, numbers for which are usually made available through crisis counseling centers (school and community), law enforcement advocates, and an internet search of "near me" options.

- **aRIFT+ Warrior Project Resources**
  Find trusted trauma-informed guidance—including resources, support groups, local aRIFT+ Big Sis Circles, and coaching—t aRIFTwarriorproject.org.

NEW HABITS TAKE SOME TRAINING
a*RIFT*₊ Challenge—a 30 Day Restoration Journey

Picture this: you end up rediscovering a place of mental freedom and self-worth you never imagined experiencing again after just one month of simple reflections and simpler changes. Close your eyes. Visualize yourself standing in a field, bursting with freedom. Are you imagining it? You can find your way to this place and begin to live there by investing about ten minutes every day for thirty days. It won't be the end of your journey, but you will be amazed at what you can accomplish in a month's time. I know some of you have doubts about experiencing such significant results in such a short time, but there's all sorts of science to back this up. Research published in "Positive and Negative Life Changes Following Sexual Assault" reveals that assault survivors—a whopping 91% of them—report experiencing improvements in their quality of life just two weeks after their assault (Frazier, Conlon, and Glaser 2001). Survivors made such progress after they intentionally worked on regaining their quality of life and rebuilding their self-worth during those initial post-attack weeks. The findings even showed similar positive changes in the twelve months following an assault. Much like the recovery processes outlined in this research, the strategies survivors used to aid their recovery were unique to each situation. There was no one-size-fits-all way to improving quality of life. They had to discover and use what was most impacting for their healing process. Yet, what strikes me here is that this speaks to considerable progress in just two weeks. Imagine what can happen in double this time.

The premise of the Restoration Journey is more than a thirty-day challenge to reset yourself. I built the challenge model around the thirty-day concept because research shows people can wrap their minds *and* hearts around a monthlong commitment. Consider how patterns of repetition, keeping time with your current timelines, and resetting yourself when you get off track all work to restore and reprogram your habits and behaviors. The practices within this challenge are built with these elements in mind and thus become the gifts that keep on giving.

Patterns of repetition are what lead to successful lifestyle changes. Beyond this, there are some distinct reasons the monthlong journey makes sense for an assault-recovery initiative. Whether it's discovering optimal coping skills, learning how to clean up your life, or learning how to live a certain way for the first time, some level of reprogramming must happen for you to enter this new or renewed existence. For these reasons, the **aRIFT₊ 30-Day Restoration Journey** revolves around the same weekly pattern with daily focuses and activities that allow you the freedom to choose how to initiate and execute each focus.

You may be thinking, why a weekly pattern? A weekly pattern is already a part of our regular life management. We use calendars to keep all the things in our lives and the larger world organized. Regardless of the method used for calendar management, there are some general concepts we learn early in life and practice throughout our lifetimes. We see a month as a whole, view a week at a glance, and handle things a day at a time. The thirty-day challenge model handles time the same way. The thirty-day challenge is the whole journey. The weekly patterns are at a glance. Each day must be executed within that twenty-four hours, not before or after.

The patterns of repetition repeat every week. Day 1 has a distinct focus, as does each respective day that follows. Day 8 then returns to Day 1's focus and repeats the pattern. The repeating pattern is designed with a twofold vision. The first is that it will guide you along your recovery journey and lead toward that freedom place. The second is that it will become a part of your intentional way of living and navigating your lifelong journey. Ultimately, the weekly pattern is meant to be adopted as a lifestyle change. This said, there is another challenge that isolates the weeklong pattern: the **Recharge 7-Day Journey**, which resets your lifelong journey when you get off track. In essence, the challenge structure invites you to live every week like a recharge week.

Each day's initiative varies and includes reflections, small changes, and actions. Because accountability is a large part of maintaining and finishing any challenge or journey, there is a journal component for each day. How you journal about your day isn't as important as the activity of writing what you will commit to your day or recording the results from your experience during the day's activity. Don't underestimate this disciplined exercise. Trust me when I say there is power, accountability, *and* inspiration in this simple act. The journaling component may also help you write through your grief stages, maybe even offering you ways to connect aspects of your grief to that day's objective. Keep in mind, connecting each day's objective to any grief stages you're dealing with is essential to working through your trauma. Use and adjust the journal section to best fit your needs.

The thirty-day structure is built on a four-week cycle of twenty-eight days with a start-up and wrap-up day. The seven-day journey follows prompts from Days 1 through 7. Thus, there are nine essential days to keep in mind. The official first day of the thirty-day journey is the start-up day, and day thirty is the wrap-up day. The next section shows an at-a-glance outline for the nine essential days. Actual initiatives and ideas for how to execute each of these days are broken down in the section that follows this:

Recovery Initiative Ideas and Prompts.

Approach your journey like a self-directed process where you have unlimited options and inspiration for how to execute your recovery days. You'll likely notice how one day's focus naturally leads you into the next day's. That's because your subconscious is doing wonderful work even when you're resting. We experience so much healing and personal insights when these patterns form and blend together. For this reason, I urge you to consider following the suggested patterns in place of picking random, unconnected daily focuses. Sometimes changing things up and following a digression is healthy in its own right. Just remember you're on a recovery and restoration journey. The path you take and the provisions you carry should logically lead you toward your end goal(s). Even digressions should allow you a way back to the path. Do you follow me here?

Start-Up Day

Think of your **Start-Up Day** as the day you develop a vision and focus for your thirty-day journey, along with what you expect to get from your experience. Here's your opportunity to make a list of your short-term and long-term goals for your recovery and life thereafter. This step is vital at the onset of your recovery journey. Like anything else in life for which you want lasting, life-altering results, you must be intentional from the very beginning. You must have an action plan and mission for how to execute it. This reflective step helps you identify what you specifically want and how you see yourself getting it. It becomes a list you can revisit during your journey, which guides you on your unique daily process toward your recovery. If you're a faith person, this list with all its specificity also acts as a confession of your current and future desires, which you can lift up in prayer and petition.

Start-Up Day initiatives and ideas are listed in the **Recovery Initiative Ideas and Prompts** section.

Day 1 is Pay-It-Forward Day

This day is about intentionally offering another person an act of kindness. This is more than the surface idea of extending kindness to receive it back. You may be surprised to learn that helping someone else—even while you need help yourself—is an effective way to rebuild your own sense of power. You don't have to pay for someone's items at the register or drive-through, either. While these acts are inspiring and uplifting, their focus is on meeting someone's financial and/or resource needs. Your approach in this step should directly correlate with your own set of recovery needs. The acts of kindness that better focus on your recovery to healthy self-worth, empowerment, and freedom don't necessarily have a price tag attached to them. There are many invisible needs you can meet for others—needs you hope someone will meet for you at some point. These might be in the form of words, deeds, time, or gestures.

Why begin your journey with paying forward an act of kindness, you might wonder? Because modeling the very behaviors you need reciprocated is one of the keys to successful recovery. Some of these invisible needs directly relate to your own invisible needs to rebuild or reinforce your self-worth, confidence, and autonomy. When deciding your act of kindness, consider the areas in your own life you need to rebuild or reinforce. Then bless others EXACTLY as you hope to be blessed. Be intentional about the acts of kindness cycle you establish. Consider this your love language for the world you inhabit. Speak this love language fluently so it comes back to you in your own dialect.

Find **Day 1** initiatives and ideas in the **Recovery Initiative Ideas and Prompts** section.

Day 2 is Self-Love Day

This day is about investing in yourself because, let's face it, you need to fuel up at the beginning of any journey. Don't skip this exercise or skimp out on it like you're simply checking something off your list. What you do to invest in yourself is a direct reflection of how you value your self-worth. If you struggle to see your full value and importance in your immediate world, this will show in all the other daily exercises. It's okay if you struggle in this area—many of us have. If this is a weaker area in your personal life, now is the perfect time to do a little training to build yourself back up again. Trust me, everyone, including you, benefits immensely in the aftermath of your personal investment in self.

Years ago, I stopped investing in self-love and lost my identity in the process. Then one day, a friend asked a simple question that reawakened something in me. She and I were discussing how stressful life had become. At the time, I was a work-at-home mom and business partner to my husband. My world had shrunk to fit into the small bubble that contained our home. Anytime I got to travel outside my bubble was supposed to be a chance to breathe some fresh air. However, I felt like I was going through my daily motions in a fog.

I'd just come from a family gathering where someone attacked my parenting prowess because my kids didn't want to sit still. To be fair, it was a nice day out and my kids didn't want to be stuck inside in front of board games and TV while the adults chattered. They wanted to be outside playing in the front yard and exploring the neighborhood on sidewalks, which we didn't have in our country life. But we all remained indoors, and at the end of our visit, I was called a bad mom for my antsy kids. This, even though I didn't give my kids what they needed and wanted most because the adults wanted other things. I was crushed by this criticism even though it seemed so illogical the more I thought about it.

"I'm doing my best for everyone around me," I told a friend. "And yet, it's never enough."

"What is it *you* want for yourself?" my friend asked.

I remember thinking, *Is she for real? I have three small kids and a family business to run. There's no room for self.* Then it hit me like a flash flood. This emptiness I felt and the fog I waded through were there because I'd erased myself.

My friend watched this realization wash through my expression. "You're no good to anyone if you're no good to yourself," she said. "Make time to take care of yourself like your life depends on it because it does."

I thought back to my antsy kids. In their childlike

wonder, their quest for self-love was instinctual, and their self-worth radiated throughout their entire beings when these needs were met. Like my kids, I come alive when I get off my butt and do something physical. When physical activity engages my mind, it's like an electric bolt charges through my body and energizes me for days.

Since this encounter with my friend, I've invested in this area of my life, and it's made a difference in all aspects of my life. I call my self-love activities *Escape Artist Antics* because I do often feel like I'm secretly running away from my daily pressures and obligations when there's clearly no time to do so. Rather than filling me with guilt, it amuses me to pull off time for self-love activities. And I have fun with it whenever I can. If, for instance, I must run business or household errands, I sometimes load my paddleboard into my car's trunk and disappear on the local lake for a half hour along the way. Other times, in the middle of grading student work or working on a freelance project, I'll stop mid task and sneak out for a run or do laps in my pool. I've even adopted these same antics in my social life. For me, this has become the best way I know to nurture the self-love areas in my life. With each act, I continue to fill myself with internal peace that takes the edge off getting through a day or something bogging me down. The trick for success is discovering what acts and/or antics will fill your own self-love needs.

Find **Day 2** initiatives and ideas in the **Recovery Initiative Ideas and Prompts** section.

Day 3 is Talk-It-Out Day

This day is about getting something off your chest, releasing something that plagues you or holds you back from living in freedom. There are many ways to talk something out. This can be a private moment between you and your journal. It can be a one-on-one or group interaction where you share it with a professional or support group in a face-to-face or digital setting. Or it can be a more intimate exchange with someone who knows you well and whose response will be informed by such knowledge. The objective is to achieve catharsis, relinquish your hold on a personal struggle, and, *if invited*, receive insights from those listening.

While the private exchange is often the initial route assault survivors gravitate toward, most of us need human interaction, especially when dealing with a trauma. In my experience, it's only a matter of time before you find more comfort and restoration when talking it out with others. This doesn't even have to be a deep discussion. Focusing on a single, small detail that you wish to see and respond to differently can have a major impact on your recovery and quality of life.

Find **Day 3** initiatives and ideas in the **Recovery Initiative Ideas and Prompts** section.

Day 4 is Walk-It-Out Day

This day is about exercising your response reaction and defense skills. Whether it's mental agility or physical strength you're after, coping with and moving beyond the devastating effects of your assault require practice. This exercise is about intentional practice intended to strengthen your coping skills so you can literally and figuratively move beyond the things that have traumatized you.

How much time you commit to this step is less important than the quality of your actions. You may decide to use this day to activate something you discovered or discussed the previous day, in your first day's reflections, or any other day in your journey. Completing this step may take you only a few minutes, but it could require more time and energy over a longer time frame. Whatever you choose to do to walk it out may corelate with any other day in your journey. It may also relate to something less specific or even to something you listed that impacts your recovery.

Find **Day 4** initiatives and ideas in the **Recovery Initiative Ideas and Prompts** section.

Day 5 is Confront-Fear Day

This day is about confronting a fear. You read that right. But don't panic. This is a go-at-your-own-pace confrontation. Fear fills us with dread because it's usually linked to beliefs that our physical and/or emotional safety are threatened. This may or may not be a rational response. When trauma enters our lives, all our fears are heightened, whether they're triggered by the traumatic experience or not. After you experience an assault, you may inherit a whole new set of fears along with some that resurface or magnify.

One of the best ways I know to build and rebuild confidence is to work through a task that has a fear factor attached to it. It takes courage to face a fear, no matter how small. Remember that heroism concept I mentioned earlier? Well, heroines dare to do difficult and challenging things because they know they must push past the obstacles holding them back from what they want or need to accomplish. They may even tremble, flinch, cringe, or take a step back. Then, they mentally regroup and get back to the necessary work before them.

What I'm asking you to do here is pick something that holds you back in any way—big, small, or anywhere in between. Confronting something you fear doesn't have to be a go-big-or-go-home kind of deal. While it's great if you decide to face one of your greatest fears, it's not a requirement for success. If you're dealing with a fear you're not ready to confront yet, start with something smaller. The idea here is to do *something*. If you totally conquer this fear, excellent. If you simply confront it and it still trips you up, be encouraged by the courage it took to interact with a fear that normally holds you back or, worse, renders you inactive altogether.

You may decide to keep coming back to the same fear or pick new ones each week. I've experienced amazing breakthroughs by dealing with one fear in stages over time. The initial step might be mentally regrouping. The next week, I might be ready to step toward it only to flinch away. The following week I take another step and remain there despite the chill that electrifies all my neck hairs. Sometimes I make it all the way through the task and never get past that chill stage. And I call this a victory because the goal is to push past the fear, not overcome the alarm it sounds while I do it. After all, sometimes these alarms are good and act as our body's way of warning us to proceed with caution.

Find **Day 5** initiatives and ideas in the **Recovery Initiative Ideas and Prompts** section.

Day 6 is Nesting Day

This day is about cleaning up, clearing out, and reorganizing life matters and/or perceptions, especially those that aren't useful or healthy for your life and future goals. Sometimes we outgrow attitudes like we outgrow that sweater we just had to buy but only wore twice. Other times we realize after some reflection that we never should have brought a certain attitude, behavior, or outlook into our life. We may even inherit (and hold on to) an attitude, belief, or outlook from our assault that serves no other purpose than to hurt or hold us back from living a healthy life. There's no good reason to let non-useful things sit around and take up wasted space in our lives. Whether it's figurative or physical items, use this day to do some important and necessary cleaning.

I find a nesting day is sometimes in order after a confront-your-fears day because you often uncover some junk thoughts and sensitivities on Day 5. While you don't have to interlink your day-to-day items, be mindful of patterns that make sense to build on. Day 6 often builds on previous focuses because you will uncover or discover things during the week that then need to be cleaned up or out of your life.

Your nesting activity could be turning a figurative item into a physical one that you can purge from your life. There's a purging activity that's a go-to for me because it offers such a physical release as I figuratively clean out and then literally get rid of something plaguing me. I call it **Meet Me at the Edge**. The concept is simple. First, you identify something putting you over the edge, troubling you, holding you back, or even debilitating you. Next, give this thing a name, write it on a physical object, and cast that object from your life. I carry a Sharpie in my purse for just such occasions. A rock, leaf, or stick are perfect items to attach my troubling thing to and then release it back to nature. There's nothing like throwing a rock far out into the lake and imagining the thing that was holding me back sinking to the lakebed. Sometimes I write my item on a recycled piece of paper before I feed it to our Franklin stove—then watch it go up in flames. The options are endless if you really use your imagination.

Find more **Day 6** initiatives and ideas in the **Recovery Initiative Ideas and Prompts** section.

Day 7 is Rest-and-Recharge Day

This day is about resting while reflecting and recharging your battery for the next week. You're no good to yourself or anyone around you if you burn out and push through your days mentally and physically exhausted. To perform at your best, you need rest. Make time to relax from the activities that physically and psychologically drain you. Spend time reflecting on the past week and meditating on how you'll recharge your focus for the following week. If prayer is a part of your life, take your reflections and meditations to God.

This reflective time is a chance to assess what went well and what didn't during your recovery week. Perhaps you have some victories to celebrate. Or setbacks. Or things you'll do differently for more specific results. Here's your chance to affirm your progress and decide to take future action if different action is needed. Then, once you release these things from your conscience, find rest in the release.

Find **Day 7** initiatives and ideas in the **Recovery Initiative Ideas and Prompts** section.

WRAP-UP DAY (DAY 30)

The final day of the **30-Day Restoration Journey** is your chance to review and reflect on your total journey and progress. Let's face it: things changed during the month—things you couldn't predict on that initial day. In light of your evolution, you'll need to revisit your Start-Up Day list of short-term and long-term goals. Then, there are several ways to assess your recovery journey and adjust your vision for life thereafter.

Find **Wrap-Up Day** initiatives and assessment strategies in the **Recovery Initiative Ideas and Prompts** section.

RECHARGE 7-DAY JOURNEY CHALLENGE

The **Recharge 7-Day Journey** is one you can adopt as a lifestyle or simply revisit when needed. In essence, the recharge week can work to keep you on track for life-long self-care or to reset your lifelong journey when you get off track. The journey challenge simply relies on the Day 1 through Day 7 focuses and initiatives. While this challenge structure invites you to live each week like a recharge week, you might find it most useful to revisit the total structure on occasion.

What you'll discover is that you will develop healthy self-care habits during the 30-Day Restoration Journey that you will continue to incorporate into your daily life. These habits may not follow a prescribed pattern or single strategy, and that's okay. For instance, you may combine several focuses and initiatives into each day, forming your own unique patterns that best fit your life-style. This is how the challenge structure has impacted my life. Yet even with this new daily approach and out-look, sometimes certain focuses will fall off your radar or become less important. For this reason, a structured recharge week is a powerful way to re-ground your focus in all areas and help you identify what's holding you back or minimizing your total quality of life. Depending on the situation, you may even need to work in a Start-Up and Wrap-Up Day to better help you identify what you hope to accomplish during your recharge. The trick is to figure out what works for you and to keep tweaking it along your life journey. Look at it this way: you have your whole life to figure out your optimal pattern.

RECOVERY INITIATIVE IDEAS AND PROMPTS

To recap, the assault grief trauma stages are shock and denial, pain, recall, guilt and shame, anger, depression, acceptance and hope, and recovery. This section contains some ideas, strategies, and prompts you may find useful when planning your challenge days. These idea lists are in no way all-inclusive. There are endless strategies and initiatives you can implement during your recovery challenge and the days that follow it. Let these inspire you where they can and come up with your own as you're led to do so. You can also visit aRIFTwarriorproject. org to view an up-to-date and evolving list of ideas and prompts.

What follows are some ways to plan and execute your challenge days. You may notice some prompts are repeated or similar to those outlined in other days. This is because many strategies are interpretive and fit a variety of objectives that exist in the different days. Your journey is your own and you should use what's helpful, even if you choose similar activities throughout the week.

As a bonus to you visual individuals who like to record your progress and journey, there's an interactive map at the back of this book. If this appeals to you, log your steps, successes, and goals as you go. Invent your own ways to mark your unique journey with pen, marker, stickers—whatever you want. Any way you proceed, may your journey to restoration be blessed with breakthroughs and personal growth.

Day 1—Pay It Forward—Strategies & Prompts

If you're dealing with a grief stage, consider paying it forward in a way that directly connects to this grief area. To recap, the assault grief trauma stages are shock and denial, recall, guilt and shame, anger, depression, acceptance and hope, and recovery. Think about where you are in your recovery journey and what your own personal needs are on this day.

Sometimes your needs might be as simple as hearing some encouragement. And if you need to hear or see something encouraging, chances are others do, too. Try being intentional with compliments throughout your day. Tack notes to public bathroom mirrors, windows, walls, lockers, message boards, building or business entrances, and/or any place you know has traffic for which your message applies. Hand them out to people personally in passing.

Let's say you're dealing with shock and denial. Speaking into shock and denial can be as easy as posting a note saying:

- You're more valuable than the bad things that happen to you.
- When you hurt, we all hurt. Know you're loved.
- You are wonderfully made.

Speaking into guilt and shame might manifest as:

- You're not responsible for another person's actions toward you.
- You're an inspiration exactly as you are.

A more general message could read:

- Your smile is the sun in my universe.
- Your new chapter begins right now.

Words may be the last thing you need today. Perhaps your needs are material. Perhaps they're physical. You could use this day as an opportunity to clean out things you no longer use—clothes, shoes, accessories—and donate them to a local crisis center or trafficking outreach. Are your thoughts what are cluttered in your life? You could pick up litter, imagining you're pitching a bad thought in the process. You could donate time in your community by dropping off some goodies at a facility or outreach center. Homemade/store-bought cookies or chocolates are great, and so are handwritten cards or other simple items that remind people they're valued. Maybe you are about to see someone during your daily activities. You could leave this person a note, thanking them for something or offering encouragement. You could also volunteer at one of these community places, even if it's only for a brief time. Maybe you've read a good book that has helped or inspired you. Consider leaving it somewhere in public with a note that says FREE BOOK.

Your physical needs may manifest as a desire for touch or being listened to. Though you might not want to hug everyone you pass, perhaps a symbolic approach of handing out Hershey Hugs to your teachers, friends, the clerk at checkout, or the receptionist at your gym or doctor's office will be just as fulfilling. Don't want to deal with people? Consider stopping by an animal shelter, rescue farm, or pet store and petting some lonely animals. This is personally one of my favorite pay-it-forward therapies, as is offering to walk someone's dog. Maybe you decide to really listen to someone when your paths are already crossing. You might be surprised at how impactful this simple act is on both the speaker and listener.

There are far more strategies than can be listed or highlighted here. You know your own life and needs better than anyone. Think about these needs and consider what you're actually able to offer at this stage in your recovery. It's okay to start with something small and simple if that's all you can manage. This is a go-at-your-own-pace journey, even though you will likely be challenged to take a step or two out of your comfort zone from time to time.

Day 2: Self-Love Strategies & Prompts

Self-love is vital to your recovery journey and life beyond it. Like every other day in this challenge, only you know what areas in your life need some loving care. Think of this as an investment you can't afford not to make, whether it costs you money, time, energy, resources, or any combination of these. Maybe you adopt my escape-artist antics. Maybe your self-love will come in the form of some physical activity you love. Or maybe it will be an act of kindness, taking time to do something for yourself that you normally don't make time to do. It could be indulging in something, but it doesn't have to cost a thing. Here are some ideas to get you started:

• Do something kind for yourself.

> • Get or give yourself a manicure, pedicure, a facial, hair treatment, or massage.

> • Spend time in meditation to clear your mind of stress and worries.

> • Take a nap or break where you do absolutely nothing but (fill in the blank).

> • Give yourself permission to say "no" to something you don't feel like doing or that you know you must do but can postpone.

> • Listen to music, a podcast, or audiobook that uplifts your spirits.

• Do something by yourself or with someone you enjoy spending time with.

> • Spend time alone in nature or in another atmosphere that inspires you.

> • Pursue an activity you enjoy, such as seeing a movie, going for a hike, learning a new skill/hobby, reading, revisiting an existing hobby/activity, crafting, or exercising.

• Find a fitting affirmation for this day and time in your recovery journey.

> • Repeat your phrase, quote, proverb, or scripture throughout the day (or week) and leave it as a note in places you'll be sure to see it.

• Do something today—anything for as long as you want—that simply makes you happy.

Day 3: Talk It Out Strategies & Prompts

Think of this step like a detox activity, where you cleanse toxins from your system. What's important here is the figurative release that leads to a literal one. For instance, if your thoughts are cluttered or bogged down with a bad or uncomfortable feeling, experience, or idea, you need a cleanse so healthy thoughts can fill this space. This step is a chance to take some weight off your shoulders by releasing something that troubles you. This activity may also be used to receive insights from someone else on this troubling thing.

There's another reason you should take this step seriously. In addition to exposing things that need cleansing, this step also helps you identify the full context of your trauma and responses to it. Without context, it's nearly impossible to assess and address the things holding you back from healing and living in total freedom. Both journaling and talking to someone offer you ways to give context to your feelings.

• Commit to a private, but focused, moment between you and your journal.

> • Freewrite to make sense of trauma and its impact on you.

> • Write to uncover, evaluate, and better understand the unpleasant experience so you can reveal levels of loss, what these mean in your life, and your role in this experience.

> • Write to identify post-traumatic stress reactions so that you can diminish everyday triggers.

> • Write to identify and then avoid overexposure to things or thoughts that only torment.

> • Write to work through and debunk guilt and shame items—realign with truth.

• Consider art therapy—solo or in a group.

> • Creatively express or expel what's troubling you or holding you back rather than doing so through words by preparing your nesting items (see **Meet Me at the Edge** ideas in the **Day 6: Nesting** section).

• Opt for a one-on-one or group interaction where you share with a professional or support group.

• Have a more intimate exchange with someone who knows you well and whose response will be informed by such knowledge.

> • Consider talking to a parent, caregiver, family member, or friend.

• If talking to a parent, caregiver, family member, or friend isn't an option, seek another trustworthy adult, which may be someone in your school's counseling or crisis center, a teacher, or someone you connect with via the resources listed in the professionally guided section.

• Confess your troubles or secrets in prayer, meditation, or even to a pet.

• Speak it aloud to your reflection in the mirror.

Day 4: Walk It Out Strategies & Prompts

Whether it's mental agility or physical strength you're after, coping with and moving beyond the devastating effects of your assault and/or its aftermath require training. For this exercise and habit, you may invest just a few minutes a day or commit to an activity that requires a longer commitment of time and energy. This is for you to decide.

If you're using this day to put some things to action you discussed the previous day or on the first day reflections, what you decide here will naturally corelate with this. If this is the case, simply follow through with an action you already started. For instance, if you prepared something for donation the previous day, use today to go take it to a donation drop-off center or women's shelter.

If you're considering something less specific that has more to do with your overall recovery journey, think about:

• If there is a behavior or attitude you're working to resolve or break, do something that tests your new response to this thing.

• If there is an activity or action you planned to engage in, make time today to do it.

 • If you considered a martial arts or defense class, sign up and attend a session. Check with your local community center, law enforcement, or school for free or low cost opportunities near you.

 • If you intend to invest in others, like volunteering at a community center of food kitchen, get out there and do it.

• If you have been meditating on a specific aspect or detail in your life, this might be a good time to speak about it aloud by bringing an affirmation into your week and journey.

 • Find a word, phrase, quote, proverb, or scripture that applies to this area of thinking, repeat it throughout the day (or week), and leave it as a note in places you'll be sure to see it. Better yet, look yourself in the eye in a mirror and say it to your reflection.

Day 5: Confront Fear Strategies & Prompts

Building and rebuilding confidence is a very personal process. However, getting there always requires working through a task that has a fear factor attached to it. This may not necessarily resolve the fear entirely, but it will build your confidence, helping you believe in your ability to function with the fear present and potentially dull or dissolve the fear down the road. You may still be identifying your fears and need to do some mental work before you can implement physical steps. Here are some ways to deal with and/or combat a fear:

• Go through with an action or activity where the fear is present, despite this fear factor.

- Consider a small step or action to confront or navigate around a fear rather than a giant, risky leap—think momentum building and expanding your comfort zone versus total and instant fear shattering.

- Mentally confront a fear by analyzing or journaling how this fear holds you back and brainstorming how you can move beyond it, move despite it, or overcome it altogether (which you can then implement on a walk-it-out day).

- Mentally confront a fear by identifying and acknowledging that it exists in your body and mind, turning it from an abstraction into the very real form it inhabits.

- Research or read about your fear to learn and find inspiration to cope with it.

- Focus on a fear that has nothing to do with your recovery.

    - Unrelated fears may be heightened by your trauma, so it's just as impactful to address these during your confidence rebuilding moments.

Day 6: Nesting Strategies & Prompts

Today is a chance to literally or figuratively clean up and reorganize life matters and/or perceptions. Be intentional here, even if it's just to get a better handle on the simpler parts of your everyday life.

Literal cleanups are powerful ways to mentally declutter and recharge. Literal cleanups also present great opportunities to prepare unneeded or unwanted items for donation or to gift them to someone who could use them. Don't underestimate a little spring cleaning and nesting. Below are some ways to approach this.

• Clean out some area in your living space like a closet, dresser, or other area filled with things you no longer wear or use or that is so cluttered you can't find your way through it.

• Reorganize or rearrange an area or room in your living space.

• Do some garden or yard work.

• Tidy or clean out your car.

• Offer to help someone else clean any of the above.

There are also many figurative mental and psychological nesting activities, including building on patterns from previous days. For instance, what you do today could set you up for what you do on your next **Day 4: Walk It Out**. In the same respect, what you opt to do on this week's **Day 3: Talk It Out** could set you up for your Day 6 next steps. Mental and psychological cleanups are an important part of maintaining your mental health and overall well-being. There's also something empowering about figurative cleanups. They're perfect for reorganizing or reprogramming life matters and perceptions because they uncover junk thoughts and sensitivities. There are so many stages of figurative cleanups, from identifying thoughts and feelings, to working through ways they hold you back, to completely overcoming, dealing with, or removing them from your life. For these reasons, the following prompts and strategies are broken into categories.

Identify cluttered thoughts and feelings and assess their impact and necessity in your life:

• Name a mental obstacle.

> • Meditate on a thought, sensitivity, or combination of them.

> • Journal about thoughts, feelings, or combination of them that you often revisit.

• Assess how your mental obstacle holds you back through meditation or journaling so you can plan ways to overcome it.

• Brainstorm how you plan to remove this internal clutter from your life.

• Create a detailed action plan, if necessary. Intentional, reasonable stages are good.

• Take action (e.g., speaking against a perception or thought throughout the day), one step at a time.

• Consider a **Meet Me at the Edge** activity by turning a figurative item (i.e., an identified trauma trigger item, attitude, behaviors or hurt) into a physical one and purging it. Here's an expanded bulleted list that builds from what's outlined in the **Day 6** section:

- Identify something putting you over the edge, troubling you, holding you back, or even debilitating you. This may or may not be related to your assault trauma.

- Name this thing and write it on a physical object.

- Consider a rock, leaf, stick, seashell, or other nature item. Just pick something nature has discarded rather than defacing something or littering.

- Use paper (loose-leaf, recycled, napkin, toilet paper).

  - Cast or eliminate this object from your life by throwing, floating, burning, burying, or flushing it.

  - Consider sharing a video clip or picture of your #MeetMeAtTheEdge purge on our Tik-Tok, Facebook [@ariftwarriorproject], Instagram [@aRIFTwarriorproject], and/or Twitter [@ariftwarrior] pages.

Day 7: Rest & Recharge Strategies & Prompts

This day is important to every area of your recovery and total well-being. Seriously. Don't even think about skipping it or minimizing it. Your total recovery and lifetime journey rely on your physical and psychologic healing and healthy function. Doctors know what they're saying when they prescribe rest when an injury is healing. Failing to follow these doctors' orders leads to further injury and/or a longer recovery time. The same is true for your emotional recovery. Even if you can't dedicate an entire day to rest and recharge, you must carve out time for it.

Since this day is about resting *while* reflecting and recharging your battery for the next week, consider a rest activity that offers chances for this work to occur. Mental and physical exhaustion lead to burnout and emotional malfunction. Emotional well-being is vital to your restoration and maintenance of your health. Rest is important to total health, so you must make time to relax from physically and psychologically draining activities. Here are some ways to approach your rest and recharge day:

• Consider this mental rest two-step practice.

    • Step 1: Reflect

        • Over a quiet moment or cup of coffee/tea, reflect on the past week, month, or even year and meditate on how you'll recharge your focus for the following week and future.

        • Assess what went well and maybe not as well as expected during your recovery week.

        • Mentally celebrate victories and breakthroughs.

- Note setbacks and things you'll do differently for more specific results.

  - If mindful or spiritual meditation is how you find mental clarity and emotional calm, elect this as your reflection option, which will then guide your release and rest steps.

  - If prayer is a part of your spiritual life, take your reflections and meditations to God, which, similarly to mindful and spiritual meditation, often guide your release and rest steps.

- Step 2: Release and Rest

  - Once identified, release or pause the negative things from your conscience.

    - This may be a chance to mentally cut yourself free from something you notice is holding you back or that isn't within your control to change.

    - Release may require a more literal activity like the ones outlined in **Meet Me at the Edge**.

    - If you can't seem to cut yourself free from some negative aspect of your trauma, give yourself permission to take a mental break from thinking about it.

    - If pausing intrusive thoughts seems impossible, even when you try, consider engaging in different mental activities that change the channel on your emotional state. Redirect and/or distract your focus intentionally. A few ways are listed in the final bullets below.

- Find rest in the release or pause.

  - Literally find time to rest and catch up on lost sleep.

  - Take a break from any activities or interactions that physically and/or emotionally deplete you.

  - Read or listen to music, an audiobook, or a podcast.

  - Watch your favorite TV shows or movies.

  - Let someone do something for you or take care of you today.

Planning and Recording Your a*RIFT*₊ 30-Day Restoration Days

Because self-reflection and intentional planning are important to your recovery and restoration, you'll need to record your experiences and thoughts for each challenge day. This section is designed for you to journal during your thirty-day journey. Each day is outlined and includes prompts. There is also an option to write in an alternate focus if you need to adjust your daily focuses throughout the week to logistically fit your schedule.

Start-Up Day:

Here's where you reflect on what you hope to accomplish over the next thirty days and some of the ways you plan to do so. It might help to list the areas where you struggle most so you're aware of these obstacles up front. Note anything that stands out to you as you work through this day's reflections. Include obstacles and/or successes you experienced as you prepared this entry. Then, make some predictions about the outcomes you anticipate at the end of this monthlong journey.

_____

_____

_____

_____

_____

_____

_____

_____

_____

_____

Day 1: Pay-It-Forward Day or alternate focus
[_____]

Note what you hope to accomplish and anything that stands out to you as you work through this day's objectives. Include obstacles and/or successes you experienced during this day, as well as anything you'd do differently in the future when you pay it forward. If you're also working through a grief stage or multiple ones, note which one(s) and how it/they impacted your focus today.

_____

_____

_____

_____

_____

_____

_____

_____

_____

_____

Day 2: Self-Love Day or alternate focus
[_____]

Note what you hope to accomplish and anything that stands out to you as you work through this day's objectives. Include obstacles and/or successes you experienced during this day, as well as anything you'd do differently in the future when you invest in self-love. If you're also working through a grief stage or multiple ones, note which one(s) and how it/they impacted your focus today.

_____

_____

_____

_____

_____

_____

_____

_____

_____

_____

Day 3: Talk It Out Day or alternate focus
[_____]

Note what you hope to accomplish and anything that stands out to you as you work through this day's objectives. Include obstacles and/or successes you experienced during this day, as well as anything you'd do differently in the future when you talk it out. If you're also working through a grief stage or multiple ones, note which one(s) and how it/they impacted your focus today.

_____

_____

_____

_____

_____

_____

_____

_____

_____

_____

Day 4: Walk-It-Out Day or alternate focus
[_____]
Note what you hope to accomplish and anything
that stands out to you as you work through this day's
objectives. Include obstacles and/or successes you
experienced during this day, as well as anything you'd do
differently in the future when you walk it out. If you're
also working through a grief stage or multiple ones, note
which one(s) and how it/they impacted your focus today.

_____

_____

_____

_____

_____

_____

_____

_____

_____

_____

Day 5: Confront-Fear Day or alternate focus
[_____]

Note what you hope to accomplish and anything that stands out to you as you work through this day's objectives. Include obstacles and/or successes you experienced during this day, as well as anything you'd do differently in the future when you confront a fear. If you're also working through a grief stage or multiple ones, note which one(s) and how it/they impacted your focus today.

_____

_____

_____

_____

_____

_____

_____

_____

_____

_____

Day 6: Nesting Day or alternate focus
[_____]

Note what you hope to accomplish and anything that stands out to you as you work through this day's objectives. Include obstacles and/or successes you experienced during this day, as well as anything you'd do differently in the future when you clean up and reorganize life matters and/or perceptions. If you're also working through a grief stage or multiple ones, note which one(s) and how it/they impacted your focus today.

_____

_____

_____

_____

_____

_____

_____

_____

_____

_____

Day 7: Rest-and-Recharge Day or alternate focus

[_____]

Note what you hope to accomplish and anything that stands out to you as you work through this day's objectives. Include obstacles and/or successes you experienced during this day, as well as anything you'd do differently in the future when you rest and recharge. If you're also working through a grief stage or multiple ones, note which one(s) and how it/they impacted your focus today.

_____

_____

_____

_____

_____

_____

_____

_____

_____

_____

Day 8: Pay-It-Forward Day or alternate focus
[_____]

What's your pay-it-forward focus this time around? Is it the same or completely different? Why? Note what you hope to accomplish and anything that stands out to you today. Include obstacles and/or successes you experienced during this day, as well as anything you'd do differently in the future when you pay it forward. If you're also working through a grief stage or multiple ones, note which one(s) and how it/they impacted your focus today.

_____

_____

_____

_____

_____

_____

_____

_____

_____

_____

Day 9: Self-Love Day or alternate focus

[_____]

What's your self-love focus this time around? Is it the same or completely different? Why? Note what you hope to accomplish and anything that stands out to you as you work through this day's objectives. Include obstacles and/or successes you experienced during this day, as well as anything you'd do differently in the future when you invest in self-love. If you're also working through a grief stage or multiple ones, note which one(s) and how it/they impacted your focus today.

_____

_____

_____

_____

_____

_____

_____

_____

_____

_____

Day 10: Talk-It-Out Day or alternate focus

[_____]

What's your talk-it-out focus this time around? Is it the same or completely different? Why? Note what you hope to accomplish and anything that stands out to you as you work through this day's objectives. Include obstacles and/or successes you experienced during this day, as well as anything you'd do differently in the future when you talk it out. If you're also working through a grief stage or multiple ones, note which one(s) and how it/they impacted your focus today.

_____

_____

_____

_____

_____

_____

_____

_____

_____

_____

Day 11: Walk-It-Out Day or alternate focus

[_____]

What's your walk-it-out focus this time around? Is it the same or completely different? Why? Note what you hope to accomplish and anything that stands out to you as you work through this day's objectives. Include obstacles and/or successes you experienced during this day, as well as anything you'd do differently in the future when you walk it out. If you're also working through a grief stage or multiple ones, note which one(s) and how it/they impacted your focus today.

_____

_____

_____

_____

_____

_____

_____

_____

_____

_____

Day 12: Confront-Fear Day or alternate focus

[_____]

What's your confronted fear focus this time around? Is it the same or completely different? Why? Note what you hope to accomplish and anything that stands out to you as you work through this day's objectives. Include obstacles and/or successes you experienced during this day, as well as anything you'd do differently in the future when you confront a fear. If you're also working through a grief stage or multiple ones, note which one(s) and how it/they impacted your focus today.

_____

_____

_____

_____

_____

_____

_____

_____

_____

_____

Day 13: Nesting Day or alternate focus
[_____]

What's your clean-up or organizational focus this time around? Is it the same or completely different? Why? Note what you hope to accomplish and anything that stands out to you as you work through this day's objectives. Include obstacles and/or successes you experienced during this day, as well as anything you'd do differently in the future when you clean up and reorganize life matters and/or perceptions. If you're also working through a grief stage or multiple ones, note which one(s) and how it/they impacted your focus today.

_____

_____

_____

_____

_____

_____

_____

_____

_____

_____

Day 14: Rest-and-Recharge Day or alternate focus
[_____]

What's your rest-and-recharge focus this time around? Is it the same or completely different? Note what you hope to accomplish and anything that stands out to you as you work through this day's objectives. Include obstacles and/or successes you experienced during this day, as well as anything you'd do differently in the future when you rest and recharge. If you're also working through a grief stage or multiple ones, note which one(s) and how it/they impacted your focus today.

_____

_____

_____

_____

_____

_____

_____

_____

_____

_____

Day 15: Pay-It-Forward Day or alternate focus
[_____]

What's your pay-it-forward focus this time around? Is it the same act you've chosen previously or different? Why? Note what you hope to accomplish and anything that stands out to you today. Include obstacles and/or successes you experienced during this day, as well as anything you'd do differently in the future when you pay it forward. If you're also working through a grief stage or multiple ones, note which one(s) and how it/they impacted your focus today.

_____

_____

_____

_____

_____

_____

_____

_____

_____

Day 16: Self-Love Day or alternate focus
[_____]

What's your self-love focus this time around? Is it the same as a previous one or different? Why? Note what you hope to accomplish and anything that stands out to you as you work through this day's objectives. Include obstacles and/or successes you experienced during this day, as well as anything you'd do differently in the future when you invest in self-love. If you're also working through a grief stage or multiple ones, note which one(s) and how it/they impacted your focus today.

_____

_____

_____

_____

_____

_____

_____

_____

_____

_____

Day 17: Talk-It-Out Day or alternate focus
[_____]

What's your talk-it-out focus this time around? Is it the same as a previous one or different? Why? Note what you hope to accomplish and anything that stands out to you as you work through this day's objectives. Include obstacles and/or successes you experienced during this day, as well as anything you'd do differently in the future when you talk it out. If you're also working through a grief stage or multiple ones, note which one(s) and how it/they impacted your focus today.

_____

_____

_____

_____

_____

_____

_____

_____

_____

_____

Day 18: Walk-It-Out Day or alternate focus

[_____]

What's your walk-it-out focus this time around? Is it the same as a previous one or different? Why? Note what you hope to accomplish and anything that stands out to you as you work through this day's objectives. Include obstacles and/or successes you experienced during this day, as well as anything you'd do differently in the future when you walk it out. If you're also working through a grief stage or multiple ones, note which one(s) and how it/they impacted your focus today.

_____

_____

_____

_____

_____

_____

_____

_____

_____

_____

Day 19: Confront-Fear Day or alternate focus
[_____]

What's your confronted fear focus this time around? Is it the same as a previous one or different? Why? Note what you hope to accomplish and anything that stands out to you as you work through this day's objectives. Include obstacles and/or successes you experienced during this day, as well as anything you'd do differently in the future when you confront a fear. If you're also working through a grief stage or multiple ones, note which one(s) and how it/they impacted your focus today.

_____

_____

_____

_____

_____

_____

_____

_____

_____

_____

Day 20: Nesting Day or alternate focus

[_____]

What's your clean-up or organizational focus this time around? Is it the same as a previous one or different? Why? Note what you hope to accomplish and anything that stands out to you as you work through this day's objectives. Include obstacles and/or successes you experienced during this day, as well as anything you'd do differently in the future when you clean up and reorganize life matters and/or perceptions. If you're also working through a grief stage or multiple ones, note which one(s) and how it/they impacted your focus today.

_____

_____

_____

_____

_____

_____

_____

_____

_____

_____

Day 21: Rest-and-Recharge Day or alternate focus
[_____]

What's your rest-and-recharge focus this time around? Is it the same as a previous one or different? Why? Note what you hope to accomplish and anything that stands out to you as you work through this day's objectives. Include obstacles and/or successes you experienced during this day, as well as anything you'd do differently in the future when you rest and recharge. If you're also working through a grief stage or multiple ones, note which one(s) and how it/they impacted your focus today.

_____

_____

_____

_____

_____

_____

_____

_____

_____

_____

Day 22: Pay-It-Forward Day or alternate focus

[_____]

What's your pay-it-forward focus this week? Is it the same act you've chosen previously or different? Why? Note what you hope to accomplish and anything that stands out to you today. Include obstacles and/or successes you experienced during this day, as well as anything you'd do differently in the future when you pay it forward. If you're also working through a grief stage or multiple ones, note which one(s) and how it/they impacted your focus today.

_____

_____

_____

_____

_____

_____

_____

_____

_____

_____

Day 23: Self-Love Day or alternate focus
[_____]
What's your self-love focus this week? Is it the same as a previous one or different? Why? Note what you hope to accomplish and anything that stands out to you as you work through this day's objectives. Include obstacles and/or successes you experienced during this day, as well as anything you'd do differently in the future when you invest in self-love. If you're also working through a grief stage or multiple ones, note which one(s) and how it/they impacted your focus today.

_____

_____

_____

_____

_____

_____

_____

_____

_____

_____

Day 24: Talk-It-Out Day or alternate focus

[_____]

What's your talk-it-out focus this week? Is it the same as a previous one or different? Why? Note what you hope to accomplish and anything that stands out to you as you work through this day's objectives. Include obstacles and/or successes you experienced during this day, as well as anything you'd do differently in the future when you talk it out. If you're also working through a grief stage or multiple ones, note which one(s) and how it/they impacted your focus today.

_____

_____

_____

_____

_____

_____

_____

_____

_____

_____

Day 25: Walk-It-Out Day or alternate focus

[_____]

What's your walk-it-out focus this week? Is it the same as a previous one or different? Why? Note what you hope to accomplish and anything that stands out to you as you work through this day's objectives. Include obstacles and/or successes you experienced during this day, as well as anything you'd do differently in the future when you walk it out. If you're also working through a grief stage or multiple ones, note which one(s) and how it/they impacted your focus today.

_____

_____

_____

_____

_____

_____

_____

_____

_____

Day 26: Confront-Fear Day or alternate focus

[_____]

What's your confronted fear focus this week? Is it the same as a previous one or different? Why? Note what you hope to accomplish and anything that stands out to you as you work through this day's objectives. Include obstacles and/or successes you experienced during this day, as well as anything you'd do differently in the future when you confront a fear. If you're also working through a grief stage or multiple ones, note which one(s) and how it/they impacted your focus today.

_____

_____

_____

_____

_____

_____

_____

_____

_____

_____

Day 27: Nesting Day or alternate focus
[_____]
What's your clean-up or organizational focus this week? Is it the same as a previous one or different? Why? Note what you hope to accomplish and anything that stands out to you as you work through this day's objectives. Include obstacles and/or successes you experienced during this day, as well as anything you'd do differently in the future when you clean up and reorganize life matters and/or perceptions. If you're also working through a grief stage or multiple ones, note which one(s) and how it/they impacted your focus today.

_____

_____

_____

_____

_____

_____

_____

_____

_____

_____

Day 28: Rest-and-Recharge Day or alternate focus
[_____]

What's your rest-and-recharge focus this week? Is it the same as a previous one or different? Why? Note what you hope to accomplish and anything that stands out to you as you work through this day's objectives. Include obstacles and/or successes you experienced during this day, as well as anything you'd do differently in the future when you rest and recharge. If you're also working through a grief stage or multiple ones, note which one(s) and how it/they impacted your focus today.

_____

_____

_____

_____

_____

_____

_____

_____

_____

_____

Final Day: Wrap-up Day

Now it's time to review your journey and reflect on your progress. Think of this as an opportunity to reassess on a larger scale and celebrate your thirty-day journey and all you accomplished. What was most helpful in your recovery process? Least? Has your list of areas you struggle with changed? How so? What else stands out to you as you worked through this challenge? What were your most challenging obstacles and most rewarding successes? In closing, how will you continue your restoration journey?

_____

_____

_____

_____

_____

_____

_____

_____

_____

_____

Recording Your a*RIFT*₊ 7-Day
Recharge Journey Days

While the thirty-day challenge structure invites you to live each week like a recharge week, you might benefit from revisiting the weekly structure on occasion. As mentioned, the Recharge 7-Day Journey can be adopted as a lifestyle or simply revisited when needed. Treat the recharge week like a reset or refresher that helps get you back on track for lifelong self-care. This recharge challenge uses the Day 1 through Day 7 focuses and initiatives.

Because self-reflection and intentional planning are important to your recovery and restoration, you'll need to record your experiences and thoughts for each challenge day in the weeklong journey as well. This section is designed for you to journal during the week. Each day is outlined and includes prompts. There is also an option to write in an alternate focus if you need to adjust your daily focuses throughout the week to logistically fit your schedule.

RECHARGE 7-DAY JOURNEY
CHALLENGE NOTES

Day 1: Pay-It-Forward Day or alternate focus

[_____]

Note what you hope to accomplish and anything that stands out to you as you work through this day's objectives. Include obstacles and/or successes you experienced during this day, as well as anything you'd do differently in the future when you pay it forward. If you're also working through a grief stage or multiple ones, note which one(s) and how it/they impacted your focus today.

_____

_____

_____

_____

_____

_____

_____

_____

_____

_____

Day 2: Self-Love Day or alternate focus
[_____]

Note what you hope to accomplish and anything that stands out to you as you work through this day's objectives. Include obstacles and/or successes you experienced during this day, as well as anything you'd do differently in the future when you invest in self-love. If you're also working through a grief stage or multiple ones, note which one(s) and how it/they impacted your focus today.

_____

_____

_____

_____

_____

_____

_____

_____

_____

Day 3: Talk-It-Out Day or alternate focus

[_____]

Note what you hope to accomplish and anything that stands out to you as you work through this day's objectives. Include obstacles and/or successes you experienced during this day, as well as anything you'd do differently in the future when you talk it out. If you're also working through a grief stage or multiple ones, note which one(s) and how it/they impacted your focus today.

_____

_____

_____

_____

_____

_____

_____

_____

_____

_____

Day 4: **Walk-It-Out Day** or alternate focus
[_____]

Note what you hope to accomplish and anything that stands out to you as you work through this day's objectives. Include obstacles and/or successes you experienced during this day, as well as anything you'd do differently in the future when you walk it out. If you're also working through a grief stage or multiple ones, note which one(s) and how it/they impacted your focus today.

_____

_____

_____

_____

_____

_____

_____

_____

_____

_____

Day 5: Confront-Fear Day or alternate focus

[_____]

Note what you hope to accomplish and anything that stands out to you as you work through this day's objectives. Include obstacles and/or successes you experienced during this day, as well as anything you'd do differently in the future when you confront a fear. If you're also working through a grief stage or multiple ones, note which one(s) and how it/they impacted your focus today.

_____

_____

_____

_____

_____

_____

_____

_____

_____

_____

Day 6: Nesting Day or alternate focus
[_____]

Note what you hope to accomplish and anything that stands out to you as you work through this day's objectives. Include obstacles and/or successes you experienced during this day, as well as anything you'd do differently in the future when you clean up and reorganize life matters and/or perceptions. If you're also working through a grief stage or multiple ones, note which one(s) and how it/they impacted your focus today.

_____

_____

_____

_____

_____

_____

_____

_____

_____

_____

Day 7: Rest-and-Recharge Day or alternate focus
[_____]

Note what you hope to accomplish and anything
that stands out to you as you work through this day's
objectives. Include obstacles and/or successes you
experienced during this day, as well as anything you'd
do differently in the future when you rest and recharge.
If you're also working through a grief stage or multiple
ones, note which one(s) and how it/they impacted your
focus today.

_____

_____

_____

_____

_____

_____

_____

_____

_____

_____

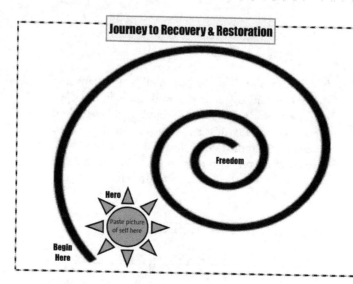

Journey to a freedom place that you reach when you spiral things into control.

Share your success story on our blog or send a snapshot of your journey board to support@aRIFTwarriorproject. org, and we'll post it in our Sister Circle.

IV
NEXT STEPS

AREAS FOR ACTIVISM
AND UPCOMING WORK

THE FIRST IN THE *LET'S TALK* SERIES

One of my works in progress in this series is *Warrior Sister, Let's Talk GIRL CODE*. In these Cancel Culture times, it's time for young girls and women to come together and rewrite SISTER CODE. *Let's Talk GIRL CODE* explores girl-on-girl bullying, gaslighting, self-censorship, and the bystander effect and how these interactions are dividing teens and young women during moments in their journey they need their sisterhood most.

The world can often feel like a cruel place to be, knocking your feet from beneath you when you're struggling to find your way and figure out who you are and want to become. If young girls and women continue to work against each other to sabotage, abuse, silence, and cancel fellow sisters—or worse, just look the other way for fear of being canceled themselves—the future looks grim. The thing is, fellow sister: a camp divided cannot conquer the world's evil forces.

If you've ever experienced bullying, gaslighting, imposed censorship, or the bystander effect—be it girl-on-girl or otherwise—let's talk about it and work together to rewrite GIRL CODE. Let's talk about (re)building a healthy thriving sisterhood where teens and young women are safe to grow into the best versions of themselves while cheering fellow sisters on in their own journeys. Warrior sister, if you're ready to change this broken GIRL CODE climate, let's get started.

An Activism Book Centered on Recognizing and Combatting Sex-Trafficking and Forced Sexual Exploitation

We live in a time when violence against and exploitation of young girls is normalized, glamorized, and made profitable. While this isn't an entirely new issue, it's one that has escalated into a whole new beast we can no longer ignore. *Warrior Sister, Cut Yourself Free from Your Assault* focuses on overcoming physical and sexual assault trauma at the individual level. My new work in progress, *Warrior Sisters, Go Back for the Girl*, is a book focused on reducing acts of violence and exploitation committed against young girls and women in more commercialized instances. As the name suggests, I'm provoking a movement to become informed warriors who take actions to help our fellow sisters who are enslaved to sexual violence and/or exploitation escape their captivity.

Woman as (sexual) object has deep roots in many cultures. The manifestation of social and power inequality runs just as deep. This power dynamic is a large influence in the patriarchal sexual order. Power equals dominance equals the one in control. From a very young age, girls are groomed and programmed to wrap their identities around their sexuality. Girls are even led to believe this is their superpower over boys and men. Boys are groomed to master the male gaze and to move from looking at pleasure objects to acquiring them. And this is only half the equation. We're such a lost society when it comes to objectifying women that we even glamorize their sexuality in death. Don't believe me? Consider the pretty dead girl trope: the centrally positioned female murder victim portrayed in forensic TV series and film. This pacified and eroticized manifestation of the dead female form perpetuates the male gaze syndrome. And this is only one example.

Let me distinguish an important point here. I am not proposing that this is about men behaving badly. Not at all. At the core of these interconnected issues is a culturally conditioned society. I believe we all play a part in this current cultural narrative. There is plenty of consensual sexual activity going on in our world and in the adult entertainment industry. Yet, there is an astronomical amount that is not. The adult entertainment industry is currently a hundred-billion-dollar industry (Polaris Project 2016) that sells sex and sexual fantasy through mass media productions and publications and through live interactions. While there is plenty of legal and consensual activity in the adult entertainment industry, it has become a perfect hiding place for distributing and selling media that contains sex-trafficked, forced sexually exploited, and underage individuals. There are an estimated 4.8 million victims who are sex-trafficked or in forced sexual exploitation in the adult sex industry, and this is just an estimate (International Labor Organization 2019). Some who engage with adult entertainment outlets that contain illicit and/or enslavement aspects aren't aware of these. Yet, others are and this is what draws them to it. What is additionally alarming about this is that there's a demand for sexual pleasure outlets that use human slaves—many underage—to deliver the desired sexual promise.

To further the depth of exploitation against girls and women, instances of sexual exploitation often entrap them in forced situations that share many traits with sex-trafficking. Initially these individuals are led to believe they're in control of their destiny in the industry. This autonomy is short-lived and quickly turns into forced sexual exploitation. They are profiled, groomed, then wrangled into entry level jobs in the industry with the promise it will lead them to the legitimate and star-like paying opportunities. First, it's modeling with a promise that the classier shoots will follow. Then, it's shot girl at the poshest gentlemen's club. Then it's, *you should be up on that stage or set making real money like those girls.* Then, *you have to work at this dumpier club until you prove yourself.* Or, *you have to do these illicit casting calls or pay a hefty fine—it's in your contract.* Pretty soon, these girls' fines are more than the new gigs coming in and they're working for free without end in sight. No matter how far they work up the adult entertainment chain, that legitimate opportunity always remains just around the corner, their big break is coming and when it does . . . Just like that, these girls become slaves to a vicious system that forcedly exploits them over and over. They are often forced into situations they didn't sign up for, at times things they specified they wouldn't do upon hire. But their debt for refusing work is in the tens of thousands and rising. And in these cases, it started off consensual. They signed on with an agent who's booking what he calls gigs. And, this agent reminds them often, they signed up for this.

The important focus here is that anyone enslaved or repressed in a forced exploitation situation deserves to be rescued from it. Those who enslave or forcibly exploit these individuals will never let them just walk away until they've made every possible dollar off their bodies. This said, there has never been a more critical time to change our socially constructed narrative. As long as one of our own is trapped in slavery or exploitation, we all should play a part in rewriting this storyline. *Warrior Sisters, Go Back for the Girl* explores the signs of sex trafficking and forced exploitation of girls and women and ways we can work together to reduce acts of violence and exploitation committed against them. If we don't break down patriarchal and socially constructed ideals that promote and enable enslavement and exploitation of and violence against women that erase their humanity, who will?

REFERENCED WORKS
AND ACKNOWLEDGEMENTS

American Association of University Women,
www.aauw.org

American Civil Liberties Union (ACLU),
www.aclu.org/title-ix-and-sexual-violenceschools

CBS News, www.cbsnews.com/news/u-s-kidssuffer-
high-rates-of-assault-and-abuse/

Crisis Text Line, Text HELLO to 741741

Equal Rights Advocates—Fighting for Women's
Equality, www.equalrights.org/legal-help/knowyour-
rights/sexual-harassment-at-school/

Frazier, P., Conlon, A., & Glaser, T. (2001).
"Positive and Negative Life Changes Following
Sexual Assault." Journal of Consulting and
Clinical Psychology, 69(6), 1048.

Gill, N. S. (8 March 2017). "Lady Justice: Justice
Goddess Themis, Dike, Astraia, or the Roman
Goddess Justicia." ThoughtCo,
https://www.thoughtco.com/lady-justice-111777

International Labour Organization,
www.ilo.org/global/topics/forced-labour/lang--en/index.
htm

Journal of Interpersonal Violence, Sage Publications,
https://journals.sagepub.com/home/jiv

Bessel A. van der Kolk, Alexander C. McFarlane, and
Lars Weisaeth, eds. (2007). *Traumatic Stress: The Effects of
Overwhelming Experience on Mind, Body, and Society.* The
Guilford Press.

Mark, Joshua J. (15 Sept. 2016). "Ma'at." World History Encyclopedia, https://www.ancient.eu/Ma%27at/

National Center for Victims of Crime, victimsofcrime.org/help-for-crime-victims/gethelp-bulletins-for-crime-victims/trauma-of-victimization

National Sexual Assault Helpline, hotline.rainn.org/online

National Sexual Violence Resource Center, www.nsvrc.org/sites/default/files/publications_nsvrc_factsheet_media-packet_statistics-aboutsexual-violence_0.pdf

National Suicide Prevention Lifeline, suicidepreventionlifeline.org/

National Women's Law Center, www.nwlc.org

Polaris Project, polarisproject.org/humantrafficking/facts

"Posttraumatic Growth Following Sexual Assault" by Patricia A. Frazier and Margit I. Berman, from *Trauma, Recovery, and Growth: Positive Psychological Perspectives on Posttraumatic Stress*, edited by Stephen Joseph and P. Alex Linley https://s3.amazonaws.com/academia.edu.documents/48922739/

Project ; Teens, projectsemicolon.com/psteens/project-semicolon-teens/

Psychology Today, www.psychologytoday.com

RAINN, www.rainn.org/statistics/campus-sexualviolence

Sutter Health Palo Alto Medical Foundation Trauma Self-Help, www.pamf.org/teen/life/trauma/

TheraPlatform, www.theraplatform.com/blog/326/psychoeducational-group-topicsU.S.

Department of Education's Office of Civil Rights (OCR), www2.ed.gov/ocr

The U.S. Department of Justice (NSOPW), www.nsopw.gov